ENTERTAINING
with
Longaberger®
CELEBRATING THE SEASONS

ENTERTAINING WITH LONGABERGER
Celebrating the Seasons
© Copyright 2003 by
The Longaberger Company
1500 East Main Street
Newark, Ohio 43055-8847
www.longaberger.com

Managing Editor:	Susie Barger
Creative Director:	Michael Kennedy
Art Director:	Jason Sigala
Project Manager:	Louann Cornell
Writer:	Mary Douglas
Project Photographer:	Colin McGuire
Corporate Photographer:	Tom Keever and Dawn Weber
Creative Style Consultant:	Keith Keegan
Food/Recipe Consultants:	Sharon Reiss and Julie Garber
Crafts/Illustration:	Patti Sharpe
Graphic Designer:	David Butler, Art of the Midwest

Library of Congress Control Number: 2003105152
ISBN: 0-9701813-3-7

Manufactured in the United States of America.
First Printing: 2003

ENTERTAINING
with
Longaberger®
CELEBRATING THE SEASONS

· Contents ·

· Welcome to Our Party ·

As America's leading maker of handcrafted baskets, Longaberger's Independent Sales Consultants host millions of home shows each year, all across the country. And since home shows are parties in a sense, we do think our experience makes us confident that we know a thing or two about hosting rewarding get-togethers.

What's more, Longaberger's original basket and pottery collections have been indispensable at almost every kind of party imaginable, in untold numbers of homes, since our Ohio-based company began in the early 1970's. In the pages ahead, you'll see just a sampling of the ways Longaberger's unique baskets, pottery, fabric accessories and wrought iron pieces can help you plan, prepare, organize, serve, store and entertain your guests in style.

We also think you'll see the versatility Longaberger can bring to your parties — and to your whole life, for that matter. Our baskets have a distinctive, honest beauty that complements the look of any room, any home and any occasion. You'll appreciate our pottery, too, for its combination of good looks and durability. Its classic design makes it as appropriate for backyard picnics as it does for dinner parties.

We dedicate this book to our family of Independent Sales Consultants, and to your family as well. We hope the entertaining celebrations on the following pages will inspire you to gather more often with friends and family, enjoying the company of loved ones and the bounty of the season.

It's time to celebrate! Won't you join us?

Tami Longaberger

PARTY PLANNING

We know you're eager to get to all the wonderful
parties in the pages ahead, but before you decide to
host one of your own, take a moment to review this
chapter. Why? Because the more you know about
planning, budgeting, invitations, menus, decorations and
serving, the more you'll relax and enjoy entertaining.
We've also thrown in lots of shortcuts for saving time,
money or both. So take a big breath and let's begin.
Good times are just ahead.

· Let's Get These Parties Started ·

Why Host A Party?

· Even if you've never hosted a party before, chances are you'll be faced with the decision to host one sometime in your life. Go ahead—say yes! You'll find that, in addition to having a surprisingly good time preparing for the party, your memories of the occasion will be that much sweeter because you created them

· People love parties as much for the camaraderie as for the simple fact that they were invited. A party invitation is a gift to a friend or loved one that says they're special enough to share in your celebration. So don't pass up any opportunity to throw a party. You'll find it's easy if you make your affection for your guests — and attention to their comfort — the focus of all your planning.

Secrets To Total Party Success:

· **Stash your serveware.** Keep platters, bowls, linens and baskets organized in one, dust-free location so they're easy to access. A large Longaberger Basket with WoodCrafts lid works nicely.

· **Lower the room temperature before your guests arrive.** Why? Because all those extra people will generate more heat. And cooler temperatures prompt guests to circulate more.

· **Guests who are sitting are guests who aren't mingling.** Provide slightly fewer chairs than guests.

· **Relax!** The best hostesses are fun, not fancy.

· Decisions, Decisions ·

ONCE YOU'VE DECIDED TO HOST A CELEBRATION OF ANY SIZE, SIT DOWN
FIRST WITH PEN AND PAPER AND MAKE A FEW DECISIONS.

1. **Draft a guest list**

   Write down the names of everyone you'd like to invite and keep the list handy. You'll probably think of a few more names to add as the date draws nearer, and you should expect some invitees to ask to bring guests. Remember, too, that typically one third to one half of the people on your guest list won't be able to attend. Bottom line: Leave plenty of room on your list for future additions and subtractions.

   If you have any flexibility in the choice of guests (meaning it's not an occasion like a family reunion or dinner with the boss), try to plan for an interesting mix of people. One rule of thumb is to dedicate half of your list to people who are already familiar with each other, and the other half to those who aren't. Also keep in mind the interests of your guests. Know that if you invite only avid golfers, the conversation will probably revolve around golf. If the majority of your guests will have nothing in common, be prepared to jumpstart conversations from time to time.

2. **Set a date and time**

   Choose a time that's convenient for you, but also check the calendar for potential conflicts for your guests. Is your party during a holiday weekend when people typically leave town? Is there a local event that might attract many of your guests? If your party is an outdoor event, check for long-term weather forecasts and schedule a date that's most likely going to be blessed with cool breezes and sunny skies.

3. **Establish a budget**

   How much are you willing and able to comfortably spend? If you don't set a reasonable budget you'll feel too out of control and stressed to enjoy anything about your party.

Jot down a list of every conceivable expense, prioritize each item and allocate funds accordingly. Don't forget to factor in extra cash to cover unforeseen expenses.

4. **Set the tone and dream up a theme**

   Will your party be casual or elegant? Intimate or all-inclusive? Inside or out? Sit-down or buffet?

   Once you've made these basic decisions, the next one is critical: What's your theme?

   A theme can be as simple as lilacs for a bridal shower, or as elaborate as a zoo-themed birthday party complete with jungle trees and wild animals.

   Once you decide on a theme, every decision is easy when you use your theme as your guideline. Let's say you're planning a birthday party for a lively teenager who loves anything Mexican. Your invitation might be a paper taco. Your centerpieces might be bowls of votive candles inside bell peppers. You might decorate with serapes and piñatas. See? Once you get the hang of it, party themes are fun!

· RSVP ·

INVITATIONS CREATE ANTICIPATION.

Timing Is Everything

It's important to send out all your invitations, or make all your phone calls, on the same day. Otherwise people on your list who get asked later may end up feeling like second choices or last-minute replacements.

If you can manage it, invitations for casual events should go out two weeks in advance. For more formal affairs, plan on three to four weeks' notice to allow guests to line up babysitters, buy gifts and find the perfect new outfit.

It's worth it to put extra thought and care into party invitations, because they can do so much more than provide the who, what, where, why and when.

Paper Invitations

Think of how you feel when you receive an invitation. You open it with a delicious sense of suspense, and read it with a growing sense of anticipation for the future event.

Invitations don't actually have to be paper, of course. They just have to be tangible. And more than any other kind of invitation, they make a party special. By their nature, they demand a higher level of commitment.

There's a bit more encouragement for guests to respond one way or another, and to attend the event if they say they will. And because paper invitations can be stuck to a refrigerator or tacked onto a bulletin board, guests can refer back to them for party details, meaning fewer guests will show up late or miss the party entirely. So if your goal is a definite head count and greater control over the planning of the party, paper invitations are the way to go.

If you do decide to send paper invitations, don't miss the opportunity to maximize their potential. Think about all the questions your guests might possibly have

when they open your invitation: What should I wear? How will I find the place? Should I bring a gift? Anticipate as many questions as you can, and answer them on your invitation. It's also an excellent idea to provide both start and end times for your party.

Your invitation is also the ideal opportunity to establish the theme of your party, and give guests enticing clues about what's to come.

Phone and E-mail Invitations

For very casual or last minute get-togethers, phone and e-mail invitations are perfectly acceptable. Be sure to ask for RSVPs, and don't expect a response rate equal to that of a traditional invitation. Don't forget to provide your phone number and e-mail address so guests can respond quickly and conveniently.

• Food, Glorious Food •

The Secret Is Simple Abundance

If you're new to entertaining and thinking about your party menu, the best advice is to stick with what you know and keep it simple. Focus on your guests and the spirit of the occasion and no one will think twice about your simple spread of cheese and crackers. Sheer abundance makes it festive, along with the care you've taken in presenting it.

If you're an old hand at entertaining, the best advice is still to stick with what you know and keep it simple. Your guests will almost always prefer your company to an impressive soufflé, and honestly, wouldn't you rather be whooping it up with them than slaving over a hot stove?

After simplicity and abundance, there are only two other important things to remember when coordinating party menus: freshness and color. The best news is it's hard to have one without the other. Think golden, crusty breads fresh from the bakery. Vibrant red gazpacho made from the freshest farmers-market tomatoes. Just-picked salad greens, and the dramatic dark purple of a warm-from-the-oven blackberry pie. Hungry yet? Your guests will be, too.

Once you've decided on your menu, but before you dash off to the grocery store, compare your menu with your guest list. Are there any kosher or vegetarian issues you need to address? Any allergies to nuts or milk? Kids with braces or aversions to anything green? You don't need to create a separate menu for every special need, but you should be certain that your menu includes enough choices to make everyone on your guest list feel welcome.

Be Ready For Anything

Keep your pantry stocked with a variety of olives, crackers, chips, nuts, fancy chocolates and beverages and you'll always be prepared for drop-in guests or larger-than-expected crowds. Every now and then, make a huge batch of cookie dough and freeze it in logs. Then watch jaws drop when you waltz out with a plate of warm, homemade cookies on very short notice.

• Staying On Budget •

SO YOU'RE IN THE MIDST OF PARTY PREPARATIONS AND FEAR YOU'RE PERILOUSLY OVER YOUR BUDGET. PANICKING DOES NO GOOD AND SIGNIFICANTLY CUTS THE FUN QUOTIENT OF THROWING A PARTY IN THE FIRST PLACE. INSTEAD, SIT DOWN AND RE-EXAMINE YOUR PRIORITIES.

1. Substitute.
With a little creative thinking, you won't have to sacrifice style to save money. Instead of hiring a DJ, hire the high school jazz band. Instead of a shrimp cocktail appetizer, substitute a Caesar salad garnished with shrimp.

2. Make Trade-Offs.
Scale back in one area and shift those savings to another area. Trade the convenience of a made-to-order dessert, for example, for one you make yourself. Forego monogrammed cocktail napkins and spend the savings on a few strings of twinkle lights.

3. Trim the List.
Expect guests to eat two of everything (two chicken skewers, two rolls, two cookies). Some guests will eat more, some less, but it's as good a way as any to estimate. Multiply the cost of that amount of food by the number of guests on your list. If the total makes you feel faint, trim your list.

4. Let friends be friends.
If they volunteer to bring flowers or dessert, let them! Be careful about asking, though. Guests shouldn't have to bear the burdens of your party.

5. Be your own florist.
Forego florist arrangements in favor of grocery store flowers you arrange yourself. Mingle a single bunch of daisies with greens from your yard and you'll not only save money, you'll get charming arrangements with a hand-touched look.

6. Borrow what you don't have.
Here's where preplanning reaps great rewards. If your menu is determined early, you'll have plenty of time to round up baskets, platters, tablecloths, extra silverware and chairs. Return everything in better condition than when you received it so friends will happily lend it again.

7. Buy in bulk.
If you're planning a very large party or a casual get-together, it can really be worth your while to purchase paper products, ice, beverages, disposables and many food items at a discount warehouse store. The cost per unit is often much lower, but only for things you know you'll be able to use without any waste. Save purchases of perishables for farmers markets or your favorite grocery store.

· Setting Up ·

TIPS FOR A TERRIFIC BUFFET TABLE.

A few days before the big day, get out every serving piece you'll be using on your buffet. Don't forget serving utensils. Now move everything around until you're satisfied with the arrangement, and then draw a quick sketch on paper to help you remember it. Put yellow sticky notes on each piece to help you remember what it will be used for. Try this little dress rehearsal once and you'll find that it vastly minimizes last-minute decisions and helps you get maximum use out of what you have. It also gives you a heads-up if you're short a piece or two, leaving you time to borrow or rent what you need.

Make sure you have ample back-up portions of everything so you can keep platters and bowls full and inviting. You may end up with lots of leftovers, but what's so bad about not cooking for the rest of the week?

Spread your tablecloth out on the table the night before the party, and mist it lightly with water. Any wrinkles should smooth out by morning.

Pull the table away from the wall so guest traffic can flow around all sides.

Give your table a sense of drama by varying the heights of the serving dishes. We like to use Longaberger wrought iron pedestals to add height, but you can achieve the same effect by slipping inverted flowerpots, small sturdy boxes or upside-down baking dishes beneath the tablecloth.

Position dinner plates where guests can pick them up first. To keep guests' hands free to serve themselves, napkins and silverware should be positioned so they'll be the last things to be picked up. Leave space on the table for guests to put down their plates while they're serving themselves, or better yet, don't have anything that requires two hands to serve.

Feature desserts on a separate table, with fresh plates, or clear your main buffet and serve desserts later.

· Getting Ready ·

CANCEL THE CLEANING CREW.

It's not necessary to deep clean every inch of your house before you throw a party; you only need to clean the areas guests will see. We guarantee no one will think less of you or your housekeeping skills if you take these simple steps a few hours before guests arrive.

1. **Attack the bathroom.**

   Your first and greatest cleaning efforts go here. The sink and toilet both need to sparkle. Hang clean towels and lay out fresh soaps. Polish the mirror. Give the floor a quick swipe. If you can, declare the room off limits until party time.

2. **Grab a big basket. Or two. Or three.**

   Take one basket into each room where guests will gather. Pile reading materials, toys and shoes into the baskets. Put the baskets in an upstairs or out-of-the-way room and shut the door. Go back to the party rooms and remove any knickknacks cluttering table surfaces. Remove any valuables, heirlooms or breakables, too.

3. **Spot cleaning saves time.**

   Clean surfaces where people will set food or drinks, and pick up any obvious debris on the floor, but don't go much beyond that. As soon as people start showing up, the floors will get dirty anyway, so why clean when no one will notice?

4. **Clean as you cook.**

   This tip is key to your sanity. When you finish using a bowl or saucepan, immediately throw it into the dishwasher, or wash it by hand and put it away. If you can, run the dishwasher and empty it before guests arrive. You'll not only keep your kitchen organized and uncluttered while you cook, you'll also have less cleanup after the party.

5. **Make a fresh first impression.**

   If you're going to splurge on only one bouquet of fresh flowers, put it in the entry hall where it's the first thing guests will see. They'll think, "How lovely" instead of, "Look at the size of those cobwebs."

· 5 PARTY-TESTED · CLEAN-UP TIPS

1. Begin the party with an empty dishwasher.

2. Line several large containers with trash bags. We like to use our Waste Baskets because they're attractive enough to use in the party area.

3. Keep one counter clear and try to confine dirty dishes to that area only.

4. Fill your sink with hot, soapy water. Toss used cooking utensils and party dishes into the sink right away. By the time you get around to washing them, the job will be practically done.

5. When guests are gone, use a large, protector-lined basket, like our Large Wash Day™ Basket, to haul dirty glassware; dishes and silverware back to the kitchen in fewer trips.

· Special Touches ·

Centerpieces don't have to be flowers—they don't even have to be fancy. Centerpieces should be an opportunity to have fun and let your creativity run wild. The only mistake is making them obstacles to conversation; make sure yours are either under 12 inches tall, or are tall enough to see under. Some ideas to get you started:

· Slip an odd number of potted plants, flowering or not, into low Longaberger Baskets®. If the pots are unattractive, tuck in backyard greenery to hide them.

· Scatter votive candles on a tray or mirror-turned-tray.

· Place a dozen or so fresh lemons in a basket or glass bowl. Polished apples or fresh artichokes are equally beautiful.

· Float thin slices of citrus in a bowl with floating candles. Leave just enough room for the candles and fruit to gently bump against each other.

· Run a short course of smooth river rocks down the length of the table, interspersed with low white candles.

· For a baby or bridal shower, make your dessert the centerpiece of your buffet. Stack cake plates in graduating sizes and arrange mini tarts, petit fours and chocolates on each tier.

· Should You Use Place Cards? ·

For seated parties, it's always a good idea to use place cards, especially if many of your guests don't know each other well. You may even ask everyone to turn their place cards around once everyone has been seated, or simply write guests' names on both sides of tented cards.

Place cards also give you control of the seating arrangement. No one knows your guests the way you do, so you're free to mix and match personalities to orchestrate the liveliest conversations. It helps to seat outgoing types in the center of the table, and more reserved guests next to those who will be most likely to draw them out. Another trick is to separate people who know each other well, but not so far that they feel alienated. Even if you don't use place cards, suggest as you're all sitting down that couples not be seated side by side, but rather across from each other.

· Light Up The Night ·

Stock up on candles when you find them on sale, because you can never have enough on hand when you entertain. Buy unscented candles to light up areas where food will be served, and scented candles to add a fragrant ambiance elsewhere.

Low light creates a cozy, intimate atmosphere, so before the party, turn down the lights if you have a dimmer switch, or turn off a few lights if you don't. Then load a tray, like Longaberger's Serve It Up!™ Basket, with an assortment of candles and walk around placing them wherever your guests will gather. Have fun lining them up on a windowsill or mantel, in groups on trays or dotting the buffet table. Be sure to protect any surfaces from dripping wax, and try to have your candles lit before guests arrive. If you'll be entertaining outdoors, light lanterns, torches and candles before the natural light fades so you won't have to take time away from your guests later. Switch on any garden lighting at this time as well.

· Breaking The Ice ·

HOW TO PUT GUESTS AT EASE SO THEY CAN CONCENTRATE ON HAVING FUN.

· When conversation lags around the table, ask: "What's the best gift you ever received?" or "What do you keep under your bed?" or "What's your dream job?"

· Instead of name cards at each place, describe each person with a word or two, like, "Jumps Out Of Airplanes," or "Tap Danced On TV." Guessing who is described on each card is as fun as finding out more details from each person.

· Put guests to work selecting music for the CD player, passing hors d'oeuvres, taking coats, wrapping silverware in napkins, filling water glasses, lighting candles—you get the idea.

· Consider beginning the party with a presentation. Ask your Longaberger Consultant to do a show, or bring in an expert on anything from Chinese cooking to flower arranging to line dancing. Make introductions first, pass drinks and nibbles, then hand over the floor. Guests will have lots to talk about afterward.

· GOOD IDEA ·

After the party, gather all of your candleholders in a basket or plastic container, and place them in the freezer. When you come back later you'll find that the frozen wax has contracted, and you'll be amazed when it pops out completely and effortlessly.

WINTER

When the weather outside is frightful, it's time to retreat to the comforts of hearth and home. At this time of year, we turn our attention inside to making the most of the holidays, with a warm-hearted Christmas morning breakfast and a candle-lit Holiday Open House. Once the holidays have passed, we invent reasons of our own to throw a party—like a beautiful fresh snowfall. Won't you join us?

·A WARM HOLIDAY· Welcome

AN OPEN HOUSE TO TOAST GOOD FRIENDS.

Because much of the focus this time of year is on gifts, it's easy to forget that this season is really all about the people in your life: co-workers, neighbors, childhood friends and family. Instead of giving each person on your holiday list a wrapped gift, why not present them, all at once, with an evening of candlelight, festive music, great food and laughter that begins with the opening of your front door? Happy holidays! Come on in!

· recipes ·

HARD TACK CANDY
SMOKED TURKEY BREAST SANDWICHES
WHITE CHEDDAR PEPPER SCONES
FRUIT *and* CHEESE PLATTER
CRABMEAT REMOULADE
SMOKED SALMON SPIRALS
WHITE CHOCOLATE PECAN FUDGE
CRANBERRY ORANGE NUT BREAD
LONGABERGER HOMESTEAD® BREAD PUDDING

· projects ·

OPEN HOUSE INVITATIONS
CHRISTMAS CANDY CONES

· getting started ·

· PLANNING TIPS ·

- Invite a high school band or church choir to perform. Express your gratitude by donating to their cause, and invite them to help themselves at the buffet.

- Have copies of the lyrics to your favorite Christmas carols on hand so guests can sing along with the band, piano, or music CD's.

- Leave instant cameras in easy reach. Affix stickers that say "Please Take Candid Pictures."

- Consider asking guests to bring hats and mittens to donate to those less fortunate. Hang them on your Christmas tree for the evening, and be sure to give them away in time to make someone's holiday warmer.

· TO DO LIST ·

- **3 Weeks Before:**
  Make and send Open House Invitations.
  Make Christmas Candy Cones.
  Prepare and freeze Cranberry Orange Nut Bread.

- **1-2 Weeks Before:**
  Purchase nonperishables.
  Fill Small Gatehouse® Basket with greenery
  for front door wreath.
  Make Spicy Plum Sauce.
  Make White Chocolate Pecan Fudge.

- **1-2 Days Before:**
  Purchase perishables.
  Set buffet table and coffee bar.
  Make Orange Jalapeño Mustard Sauce.
  Make Dilled Crème Fraiche.
  Make Smoked Salmon Spirals.
  Make Longaberger Homestead® Bread Pudding.

- **Party Day:**
  Defrost Cranberry Orange Nut Bread in the morning.
  Make White Cheddar Pepper Scones.
  Make Crabmeat Remoulade.
  Assemble Fruit and Cheese Platter.
  Slice turkey and assemble platter.

OPEN HOUSE INVITATIONS

1. Using the red thin line marker, write your party information on one of the white panel cards. Add a watercolor sprig of holly if you're feeling festive and artistic.

2. Create the red front door:

   a. Make a miniature wreath by twisting together the ends of the garland. Set aside.

   b. Cut the shiny red paper to fit inside the recessed panel.

   c. Using the thin black marker, draw rectangles on the red paper to represent the panels on the door.

   d. Glue the red door into the recessed panel of the second white panel card.

3. Attach the wreath:

   a. Using the hole punch, punch two vertical holes at the top center of the red door, about ¼ inch apart.

   b. With the hobby knife and ruler, slice through the three sides of the door so that it opens.

   c. Thread the organza ribbon through the two holes and tie the wreath to the red door with a pretty bow. Add the optional gold bell.

4. Attach the door:

   a. Glue the four white edges of the door card onto the party information card and you will have an invitation that says "Open House" like no other!

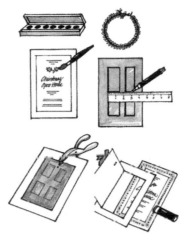

SUPPLIES

for each invitation:

White envelope

2 white panel cards

Shiny red paper

Wired miniature holiday garland

Green organza ribbon, 5/8-inch width

Black thin line marker

Red thin line marker

Red and green watercolors

Small pointed paintbrush

Ruler

Hobby knife

Scissors

Hole punch

Glue stick

Tiny gold bells, optional

CHRISTMAS CANDY CONES

Nestle these translucent paper cones in a Medium Gathering Basket or hang them from your Christmas tree. They'll look beautiful either way, and guests will love taking home these sweet mementos of your holiday open house.

1. Using a compass, draw two 6½-inch arcs on opposite corners of the vellum paper as illustrated. Cut along the line created by the compass. Place a strip of double-faced tape along the entire length of one diagonal side. Roll into a cone and press to seal.

2. Scallop the top edge of the cone with scissors. Then punch a hole into the center of each scallop.

3. Using white glue, outline the scalloped edge. Dip the wet edge into the white sugar and allow to dry.

4. Weave the ribbon through the holes starting and finishing where you would like the bow to be. Skip a hole on each side of the cone to allow for a hanging loop. Fill with Hard Tack Candy. (Recipe on next page)

· A Little Cup of Cheer ·

Votive candles in pottery Votive Cups make great, go-any-where holiday decorations. Make yours extra festive with simple rings of evergreens and berries. Put a votive beside the sink in a powder room, march a line of them across a mantel or windowsill, or scatter them on the buffet table, coffee table and end tables. Wherever you put them, be sure they're not left burning unattended.

· recipes ·

makes about 2 pounds

Ingredients:

- 3½ cups granulated cane sugar
- 1 cup light corn syrup
- 1 cup water
- 1 teaspoon clove oil, peppermint oil, cinnamon oil, or other flavoring oil (available at gourmet food and health food stores)
- 1 drop food coloring, optional
- Confectioners' sugar, optional

Instructions:

- Line a 12x17½-inch jellyroll pan with aluminum foil. Lightly mist the foil with vegetable oil spray or dust it with confectioners' sugar.
- Combine the sugar, corn syrup and water in a deep, heavy-bottom saucepan. Cook over medium heat, stirring to dissolve the sugar. Bring to a boil and stop stirring.
- Clip on a candy thermometer and cook the syrup until it reaches 310°F.
- Stir in the desired flavoring oil and optional color. (To make more than one flavor, pour half the syrup into a heatproof mixing bowl, and add a different flavor and color to each half, working quickly to keep the syrup from hardening.)
- Pour the syrup into the prepared pan. Once the candy has cooled completely, break each sheet into bite-size pieces.
- Dust with the optional confectioners' sugar. Store in an airtight container for up to 2 months.
- Though Hard Tack Candy isn't hard to make, it is extremely hot during the final stage of this recipe, so please handle it with care.

· Sweet Memories ·

Americans have enjoyed this sweet and simple recipe since the days when our country was still just an assortment of colonies. Tami and Rachel Longaberger have enjoyed it every Christmas since they can remember. They recall how their mother would boil the syrup on the stove, then remove the marble top from her dresser and pour the hot liquid candy across its smooth surface to cool.

SMOKED TURKEY BREAST SANDWICHES

Ingredients:
- One 8- to 10-pound fully cooked smoked turkey breast (available at upscale delicatessens, gourmet food stores or poultry shops)
- Orange Jalapeño Mustard Sauce
- Spicy Plum Sauce
- White Cheddar Pepper Scones, recipe on page 29

Instructions:
- Slice turkey and arrange slices on a large platter. Place sauces and condiments in small crocks, and arrange crocks either on the platter or next to it. Slice scones, rolls and biscuits; serve in baskets.

Orange Jalepeño Mustard Sauce
makes about 1½ cups

Ingredients:
- 1 cup mayonnaise
- ¼ cup whole grain mustard
- 1 large jalapeño, seeds and stem discarded, then minced
- Zest from 2 oranges, minced
- 1 teaspoon cider vinegar
- 1 tablespoon molasses
- ½ teaspoon salt

Instructions:
- Stir all ingredients together in a medium mixing bowl. Refrigerate in an airtight container. Flavor is best if sauce is made a day in advance and used within a week.

Spicy Plum Sauce
makes about 2 cups

Ingredients:
- 2 or 3 medium-size dried ancho chilies or New Mexico red chilies, stems and seeds discarded
- 1 cup chopped onion
- ¼ cup cider vinegar
- ½ teaspoon ground cloves
- ½ teaspoon ground allspice
- 1 whole garlic clove, crushed
- 2 teaspoons minced fresh ginger
- One 13-ounce jar plum jam, available at specialty food markets or larger supermarkets

Instructions:
- Soften the chilies in a bowl of very warm water for 30 minutes. Discard the water.
- Combine the chilies, onion, vinegar, cloves, allspice, garlic and ginger in a medium saucepan with 1 cup of water; bring to a boil over medium-high heat, stirring occasionally. Reduce heat to medium and simmer for 10 minutes.
- Add the plum jam and simmer for an additional 15 minutes, or until reduced by one third. Cool slightly and purée the contents of the pan in a blender. If the sauce seems thin, return it to the pan and reduce it until it has a thicker consistency.
- Cool and refrigerate in an airtight container. Sauce may be made up to 1 week in advance.
- Note: Ancho and New Mexico red chilies can be found in Latin grocery stores or larger supermarkets. Ancho chilies have a milder flavor and less heat than New Mexico chilies.

WHITE CHEDDAR PEPPER SCONES

makes 2 dozen 2-inch scones

Ingredients:

- 2 cups all-purpose flour plus extra for rolling out the dough
- 1 tablespoon baking powder
- ½ teaspoon salt
- 1 teaspoon dry mustard
- 1½ teaspoons freshly cracked black pepper
- 4 ounces sharp white cheddar cheese, grated
- 3 tablespoons unsalted butter, softened
- ¼ cup minced scallions, white and light green parts (4 or 5 scallions)
- 1¼ cups heavy cream plus extra for brushing the tops of the scones
- 2-inch circle cutter

Instructions:

- Preheat oven to 375°F.
- In a large mixing bowl, combine the flour, baking powder, salt, dry mustard and pepper. Add the cheese and butter and rub them into the flour mixture until the mixture has the consistency of coarse crumbs. Add the scallions and cream, mixing lightly just until the dough forms a ball. Press the dough into a disk.
- On a lightly floured surface, roll out the dough to a ¼-inch thickness. Use a 2-inch circle cutter to form as many scones as possible, then gently press together the leftover scraps and cut out additional circles. Place scones on an ungreased baking sheet.
- Brush tops with cream and bake 15 to 17 minutes or until light golden brown. Transfer to a cooling rack.
- Scones are best eaten the same day that they are made. To prepare sandwiches, split each scone in half and fill with a slice of smoked turkey and a slathering of Orange Jalapeño Mustard Sauce or Spicy Plum Sauce.

· GOOD IDEA ·

Homemade scones are a scrumptious addition to this holiday buffet, but yours will be just as impressive if you substitute a few varieties of good bakery rolls.

· Holidays for Heroes ·

In the years before he established The Longaberger Company, Dave Longaberger owned a small restaurant in Dresden, Ohio, named "Popeye's." ("Popeye" was his childhood nickname.) His youngest daughter, Rachel, recalls how her dad hosted a big meal at the restaurant each holiday season for the local firefighters and law enforcement officers. "It was his way of showing his appreciation for all they did during the year," says Rachel, who vividly remembers helping out at those get-togethers. "I saw first-hand my dad's commitment to his community, and it's a lesson I'll never forget."

Ingredients:

- 3 to 5 varieties of cheese (about 1 ounce of each cheese per person)
- Assorted fresh greens such as lemon, galax or grape leaves for decoration
- Apples, pears, figs, grapes, apricots, cherries or other seasonal fresh fruits
- Dried fruits such as apricots, cranberries, figs and dates
- An assortment of breads and crackers
- Platters, plates, cheese knives, and baskets

A fruit and cheese arrangement is an ideal way to enhance any buffet without additional cooking. Visit a cheese shop or a larger supermarket with a special cheese department and ask for samples to taste. Try new varieties of a favorite cheese, say, a sharper white cheddar, or an aged rather than younger Gouda.

Choose a selection that possesses contrasts: hard and soft textures; mild and stronger flavors; a variety of colors; different shapes on the plate (for instance, a white, log-shaped, soft cheese; a harder, amber-colored wedge; a yellow square riddled with "eyes"). Here's a model range: a soft, triple-cream cheese such as Saint André or a soft-ripened French Brie; a blue cheese such as Roquefort or Stilton; a semi-soft cheese such as Gouda or Jarlsberg; a semi-hard cheese such as the English cheddars that vary in texture as well as flavor; and then a harder cheese such as Spanish Manchego or California Dry Jack.

Another idea to consider is featuring cheeses from one particular country or region. For example, an Italian cheese plate might include Gorgonzola, Parmesan, pecorino and fontina.

In every case, remove the cheeses from the refrigerator two hours before serving so that they can be warm enough to reveal their peak flavor. To finish the arrangement, choose platters and baskets to display the various components. Tuck a few leaves around the cheeses for a natural look. Place the assorted fruits

around the cheeses; leaving enough room so that a guest can cut the cheeses without disturbing the entire arrangement. Fill baskets with crackers and breads (choose a variety of shapes and textures like bread sticks, flatbreads, raisin breads, small hard rolls, simple water or cream crackers, oatmeal biscuits, toasts, etc.) Place a few small knives around the platters. You can place a small card in front of each cheese to identify the type if you'd like.

If you have a little extra time, try these simple additions:

- In a covered dish, kept in the refrigerator, marinate slices of soft goat cheese in olive oil and herbs for up to a week in advance; the flavor will only increase. Serve in a shallow bowl.
- Roll a log of soft goat cheese in freshly chopped herbs or chopped pecans or walnuts.
- Peel and discard the top rind of a Brie cheese and spread the soft interior with fig jam or chutney.
- Combine equal portions of blue and cream cheese and fold in a small amount of unsweetened whipped cream for a blue cheese mousse that can be spread on crackers or breads.

CRABMEAT REMOULADE

makes 3½ cups, serves 12

Ingredients:

- 1 pound fresh backfin or lump crabmeat (available in the grocer's fresh seafood case)
- 8 ounces cream cheese
- ¼ cup mayonnaise
- ⅓ cup minced scallions, white and light green parts only
- 1 tablespoon whole grain Dijon mustard
- 4 teaspoons horseradish
- 2 teaspoons Tabasco or other favorite hot sauce
- 2 tablespoons chopped flat-leaf parsley, plus more for garnishing
- ½ teaspoon fresh tarragon, chopped, or ⅛ teaspoon dried tarragon, crumbled
- Salt and freshly cracked black pepper, to taste
- Optional garnishes:
  - Red and green bell peppers, diced
  - Hard-boiled egg whites, diced

Instructions:

- With a fork, flake the crabmeat in a small bowl; remove any shells or cartilage.
- In the bowl of an electric mixer, beat the cream cheese until smooth. Add the mayonnaise and beat again until smooth.
- Place the horseradish in a small strainer and, with the back of a spoon, press out and discard any liquid.
- Remove the bowl from the mixer and fold in the scallions, mustard, horseradish, hot sauce, parsley, tarragon and black pepper. The remoulade should be made at least 2 hours, but no more than 8 hours, before serving. Keep it in the refrigerator, covered.
- Place the chilled spread in a bowl and garnish with one or more of the options listed at left.
- Serve with small toasted French bread wedges, crackers, cucumber slices or spears of Belgian endive.

· GOOD IDEA ·

A wheel of Brie and a dozen crisp apples are nice to have on hand for this party and throughout the holidays, in case unexpected guests drop in. Peel the top off a small Brie (8-ounces) and discard the rind. Place on a microwave-safe plate and warm slightly in a microwave, about one minute. Arrange apple wedges around the Brie for dipping.

SMOKED SALMON SPIRALS

makes 30 *to* 35 *pieces*

Ingredients:

- Five 8½-inch soft lavosh flatbread rounds or flour tortillas
- 1 recipe Dilled Crème Fraîche
- 1 English (seedless) cucumber, very thinly sliced
- 1 bunch fresh watercress or 10 medium-sized romaine lettuce leaves, central ribs removed and each leaf torn in half
- 1 pound smoked salmon, thinly sliced (10 to 15 slices)
- 1 to 2 ounces salmon roe, optional, for garnish
- Fresh dill sprigs, optional, for garnish

Instructions:

- Place a lavosh on a clean cotton towel. Spread with 3 tablespoons of Dilled Crème Fraîche. Cover with a layer of cucumber, about 10 slices, not overlapping. Top with 8 to 10 sprigs of watercress. Place 2 to 3 slices (about 3 ounces total) of smoked salmon on top.
- Use the towel to lift and roll the layered bread into a tight spiral. Wrap the roll tightly in plastic wrap. Repeat with the 4 other lavosh. Place the wrapped rolls on a tray and refrigerate for at least 2 hours and up to 24 hours.
- Remove the plastic wrap and place the seam side down on a cutting board. Trim off the curved ends of each roll. Slice each roll into 6 or 7 pieces. Set them, cut side down, on a serving plate. Garnish each slice with an optional dab of salmon roe and a pinch of fresh dill.

DILLED CRÈME FRAÎCHE

Ingredients:

- 1 cup crème fraîche (sour cream may be substituted)
- 5 tablespoons chopped fresh dill or 5 teaspoons dried dill
- 4 tablespoons capers, chopped
- 2 tablespoons chopped fresh chives
- ¼ teaspoon salt
- Freshly cracked black pepper, to taste

Instructions:

- Mix together all ingredients in an airtight container. May be made 2 days in advance and stored in the refrigerator.

· GOOD TO KNOW ·

Who wants to leave the party to replenish trays? Before the party, fill a second Small Serving Tray Protector with Smoked Salmon Spirals, cover with plastic wrap and store in the refrigerator. Then, when the first batch runs out, simply pull out the empty protector and slip in the spare.

WHITE CHOCOLATE PECAN FUDGE

makes about 2½ pounds

Ingredients:

- 1½ cups pecans
- One 14-ounce can sweetened condensed milk
- 1½ pounds good-quality white chocolate, chopped (do not use white chocolate chips)
- 4 tablespoons unsalted butter
- Seeds from 1 vanilla bean (pod split lengthwise, seeds scraped free) or 2 teaspoons pure vanilla extract

Instructions:

- Preheat oven to 350°F.
- Place the pecans on a baking sheet and toast in the oven until they darken slightly, about 7 to 10 minutes. Allow the nuts to cool, then chop coarsely.
- Line an 8x8-inch baking dish with aluminum foil; allow the foil to extend beyond the edges of the pan to make it easier to lift the fudge out for cutting.
- Combine the sweetened condensed milk and butter in a medium saucepan and cook over medium-low heat until the butter has melted. Add the chopped white chocolate and stir until melted. (White chocolate burns easily; do not leave the pan unattended.)
- Remove the pan from the heat and add the vanilla seeds and the pecans. With a wooden spoon, vigorously beat the fudge for several minutes until it loses some of its glossy sheen and turns opaque.

- Pour the fudge into the prepared baking dish and smooth the top with a spatula. Cover with plastic wrap and refrigerate for at least 4 hours, or until the fudge sets.
- Using the foil "handles," lift the fudge from the pan and cut into 1-inch pieces. Store in the refrigerator for up to 1 week.

> **· VARIATIONS ·**
>
> **WHITE CHOCOLATE PEPPERMINT FUDGE**
> Substitute 1 teaspoon peppermint extract for the vanilla and 1 cup crushed peppermint candies for the pecans.
>
> **WHITE CHOCOLATE MACADAMIA NUT FUDGE**
> Replace the pecans with 1 cup chopped macadamia nuts and 1 cup toasted unsweetened coconut. Add the zest of 1 lime or 1 orange.
>
> **· GOOD TO KNOW ·**
>
> You can see in the photo below that we've placed a pottery Rectangular Tray of White Chocolate Pecan Fudge on a Longaberger Small Gathering Basket. Why? Because inside the basket is, you guessed it-more White Chocolate Pecan Fudge! Replenishments are right at your fingertips!

CRANBERRY ORANGE NUT BREAD

makes two 8½x4-inch loaves

Ingredients:
- 3 large eggs
- 2 cups granulated sugar, ¼ cup reserved for the glaze
- 1 cup vegetable oil
- 2 cups sour cream
- Zest of 2 oranges
- 3 cups all-purpose flour
- ½ teaspoon baking powder
- 1 teaspoon baking soda
- ½ teaspoon salt
- 1½ cups chopped fresh cranberries
- ½ cup chopped walnuts
- ½ cup fresh squeezed orange juice

Instructions:
- Preheat oven to 350°F. Lightly mist two 8½x4-inch loaf pans with vegetable oil spray. Line each pan with parchment paper and mist the paper with the vegetable oil.

- Whisk together the eggs and 1¾ cups sugar in a large mixing bowl. Add the oil and combine thoroughly. Stir in the sour cream and orange zest.
- Sift together the 4 dry ingredients in a bowl. Fold this mixture into the batter and stir until just incorporated. Fold in the cranberries and nuts just to combine. Pour half the batter into each prepared pan and bake for 45 to 55 minutes or until a toothpick inserted into the center of the bread comes out clean. If the top of the bread browns too quickly, loosely cover the loaf with aluminum foil. Transfer the pans to a cooling rack.
- Combine the orange juice and the reserved ¼ cup sugar in a saucepan and cook over medium heat until the sugar dissolves. Brush the glaze over the hot bread. Cool 30 minutes, and then gently remove the loaves from the pans. Cool completely.
- Covered with plastic wrap, the loaves can be refrigerated for 3 or 4 days or frozen for 1 month.

· GOOD TO KNOW ·

COFFEE, ANYONE?

Set up everything guests will need for coffee in advance-and save space on your buffet by creating a "coffee bar" with a two-tiered stand like our Small Bakers Rack™. Here it's outfitted with its optional WoodCrafts shelves, offering fresh cream, sugars, spoons and napkins. We think the coordinating baskets and pottery pieces give it gourmet glamour, don't you?

LONGABERGER HOMESTEAD® BREAD PUDDING

makes one 9x13-inch pan or 12 individual 8-ounce servings

Ingredients:

- 8 tablespoons unsalted butter, 2 tablespoons for buttering bakeware, 6 tablespoons cut into ½-inch pieces
- 1 cup pecans, for garnish
- 5 large eggs
- 2 large egg yolks
- 1½ cups granulated sugar
- 4 teaspoons pure vanilla extract
- 2 tablespoons ground cinnamon
- 5 cups whole milk
- 1½ pounds white sandwich bread with crusts, cut into ¾-inch cubes
- ¾ cup caramel sauce

Instructions:

- Preheat oven to 325°F. Generously grease the inside of a 9x13-inch baking dish or twelve 8-ounce Small Dessert Bowls with 2 tablespoons of butter.
- Place the pecans on a baking sheet and toast them for 7 to 10 minutes. Cool, chop coarsely, and reserve for garnishing.
- In a large mixing bowl, whisk together the eggs, egg yolks, sugar, vanilla and cinnamon. Stir in the milk. Add the bread cubes and the 6 tablespoons of butter pieces; toss to combine. Allow the mixture to rest for 20 minutes. Toss again and transfer to the prepared baking dish or Small Dessert Bowls.
- If using the baking dish, cover it with aluminum foil and bake for 15 minutes; remove the foil and bake an additional 20 to 25 minutes or until the top is golden brown. If using the Small Dessert Bowls, place them on a baking sheet and cover them with a sheet of aluminum foil. Bake for 15 minutes, then remove the foil and bake an additional 15 to 20 minutes.
- Allow the bread pudding to rest for 10 to 15 minutes. Slice the baking dish bread pudding into 12 portions. Place individual portions on a dessert plate. Drizzle puddings with caramel sauce, sprinkle with the reserved pecans, and serve.

- Bread pudding may be made in advance and re-warmed in a 200°F oven. Add the caramel topping and nuts just before serving.

• Always a Hit! •

This recipe is so popular with visitors to Longaberger Homestead® that nearly 2,500 servings are sold each year! In fact, our bread pudding is in such high demand that it is served in two restaurants–The Heartland Deli and The Homestead Restaurant. We hope you'll enjoy it as much as we do!

·A GOOD MORNING·
ho ho ho

OUR GIFT TO YOU—A MARVELOUS, MAKE-AHEAD, CHRISTMAS MORNING BREAKFAST.

Once Christmas Eve hits, the schedule gets tight. There are bicycles to assemble, presents to wrap, stockings to fill, and cookies to set out for Santa. Then there's the big gift exchange, perhaps church services to attend, and finally, a fabulous Christmas Dinner to share with family and friends. Who has time for breakfast? You do! Our menu features a savory casserole, an oven-baked French toast, and a refreshing fruit salad that can all be prepared ahead on Christmas Eve. Serve muffins in a basket and you'll only have three dishes to wash Christmas morning!

· recipes ·

SAVORY BREAKFAST CASSEROLE
BAKED APPLE FRENCH TOAST
BANANA CRUMB MUFFINS
CITRUS BOWL *with* VANILLA YOGURT SAUCE

· projects ·

FEATHERED FRIEND FEEDER

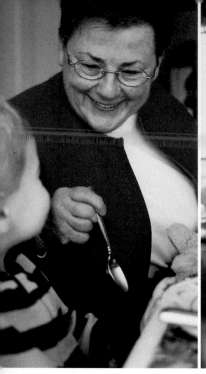

• getting started •

• PLANNING TIPS •

- Assign each of the kids a large Longaberger Basket to hold their small gifts as they are opened. The baskets keep everyone's gifts separate, little pieces don't go missing, and handles make it all easy to tote away to a bedroom or playroom.

- Ask everyone beforehand to open gift boxes without damaging them, in case you'll need to return the gift in its original box. Set aside a central place to store the boxes for at least a week or two.

- Keep all gift receipts together in a safe place, like our Address™ or Large Recipe™ Basket. The Longaberger WoodCrafts® Lid keeps the secrets hidden from prying eyes.

- To keep curious recipients from rummaging under the tree to find their presents before the big day, try this: Instead of writing names on gift tags, assign a number to everyone and write that on the tag instead. Don't tell anyone what his or her number is! Keep the number key safely hidden away (in a place you'll be sure to remember) until Christmas morning.

- **3 Weeks Before:**
  To recreate our Christmas morning centerpiece, place a tiny evergreen tree in our American Holly™ Pottery Vase, and locate a few of your favorite toys. Keep the tree well watered and display it on a side table or mantel until Christmas morning.

  Place 4" potted poinsettias in Tall Tissue™ Baskets. Keep their soil moist.

  Assemble Feathered Friend Feeders, freeze and wrap in wax paper if they're for gift giving.

- **1-2 Weeks Before:**
  Bake and freeze Banana Crumb Muffins.

- **Day Before:**
  Assemble and wrap any last-minute gifts.

  Prepare and refrigerate Savory Breakfast Casserole, Baked Apple French Toast, Citrus Bowl and Yogurt Sauce.

  Prep coffeemaker and set up morning coffee tray.

  Defrost the Banana Crumb Muffins overnight.

  Set the table for Christmas Morning breakfast.

  Place large, empty trash bags by the tree to collect discarded wrapping paper.

  Check camera batteries and make sure there's plenty of film on hand.

  Don't forget Santa's milk and cookies!

- **Christmas Morning:**
  Bake Savory Breakfast Casserole and Baked Apple French Toast while the wrapping paper is flying!

Our Centerpiece
· is Child's Play ·

It begins with a miniature tree planted in our American Holly™ Pottery Vase, surrounded with a few small toys from your past. Ask children and any grown-up guests to contribute a favorite toy, too, along with a short story to go with it. The memories evoked by the toys could very well turn this whimsical centerpiece into a much-anticipated tradition.

· Fast, Festive Flowers ·

Who needs a houseful of garland and glitz when a few fresh poinsettias make such a dramatic statement all by themselves? Streamline your decorating to-do list by picking up a few poinsettias in 4-inch pots at the start of the holiday season. Place them in something pretty, like our Tall Tissue™ Baskets shown here, give them a drink now and then, and they'll beautifully deck your halls throughout the holidays.

FEATHERED FRIEND FEEDER

SUPPLIES

Waterproof corrugated board

Silver jewelry wire

Creamy peanut butter

Three colors of birdseed, such as:
Black thistle
Ivory millet
Yellow cracked corn

Hobby knife for an adult

Wire cutter

Hole punch

Large cookie cutter, optional

1. Have an adult cut holiday shapes out of waterproof corrugated board with a hobby knife. Use a large cookie cutter as a template or draw shapes freehand.

2. Punch two holes in the top of each shape for balanced hanging. With jewelry wire, create a hanging device as plain or as elaborate as you'd like.

3. Spread creamy peanut butter evenly over the top and sides of the shape.

4. Sprinkle on birdseed one color at a time, pressing in the seeds as you go. Hang outside and watch the birds flock to their Christmas treat!

• GOOD IDEA •

These birdseed feeders make great gifts from kids to a mom, dad, grandparent or teacher. You can make them well in advance of Christmas gift-giving time, then freeze them on colorful squares of poster board. Wrap them simply, envelope style, in wax paper, and seal them closed with a holiday sticker large enough to accommodate your child's handwritten message.

SAVORY BREAKFAST CASSEROLE

serves 6 to 8

Ingredients:

- 2 tablespoons unsalted butter
- 2 large shallots, chopped (¼ cup)
- 1 pound button mushrooms, quartered
- 1 cup heavy cream
- 2½ cups dried herbed bread stuffing (cubes)
- 1 cup shredded white cheddar cheese
- 1 cup shredded sharp cheddar cheese
- 1 pound bulk mild pork or turkey sausage, cooked, drained and crumbled
- 6 large eggs
- 2½ cups whole milk
- 1 teaspoon dry mustard
- Salt and freshly cracked black pepper, to taste

Instructions:

- Melt the butter in a medium skillet over medium-high heat until it foams. Add the shallots and sauté for 2 minutes or until they are translucent. Add the mushrooms and cook for 5 to 7 minutes or until the mushrooms have released their liquid and are tender and dry.
- Add the cream, turn the heat to high, and reduce the liquid by half. Remove the sauce from the heat.
- Lightly mist a 2-quart baking dish with vegetable oil spray. Spread an even layer of cubed bread stuffing in the bottom of the pan. Combine the two cheeses and spread 1 cup of the cheese mixture over the bread layer. Add a layer of crumbled sausage and then a layer of creamed mushrooms. Beat the eggs, milk, mustard, salt and pepper in a medium mixing bowl and pour the custard over the layers. Top with the remaining cheese. Cover with plastic wrap and refrigerate overnight.
- Preheat oven to 300°F. Bake uncovered for 1 hour. If the custard hasn't completely set, bake an additional 10 to 20 minutes.

Delicious Christmas
• Traditions •

Make cutout sugar cookies on Christmas Eve, and have the whole family help decorate them. Hold a "secret ballot" vote for the best-decorated cookie, and make sure the winner is always the youngest child (declare a tie, of course, if there are multiple little ones.) Leave the winning cookie on a plate for Santa, and have "him" leave a complimentary note saying it was the most delicious cookie he's eaten all year. Now that's a delicious tradition!

BAKED APPLE FRENCH TOAST

Serves 6

Ingredients:

- 1 recipe Sautéed Apples
- 4 ounces cream cheese
- 2 ounces almond paste (available at specialty food stores or large supermarkets)
- 3 croissants (approximately 5 inches long) split horizontally
- 3 large eggs
- 1 large egg yolk
- ½ cup half-and-half
- 1 cup whole milk
- 1 tablespoon melted butter
- 1 tablespoon granulated sugar
- ¼ cup almond slices

Instructions:

- Mist an 8x8-inch baking dish with vegetable oil spray. Spread the sautéed apples across the bottom of the pan.
- Place the cream cheese and almond paste in the bowl of an electric mixer and mix until smooth. Spread 1 generous tablespoon on each croissant half. Arrange the halves, spread-side down, on top of the apples.
- In a mixing bowl, whisk together the eggs, egg yolk, half-and-half and milk. Pour the egg mixture over the croissants. Drizzle with melted butter and sprinkle with sugar and almond slices. Cover with plastic wrap and refrigerate for 6 hours or overnight.
- Preheat oven to 325°F. Replace the plastic wrap with aluminum foil and bake for 20 minutes. Uncover and bake an additional 15 to 20 minutes or until the top is a crisp, golden brown and the egg mixture has set.
- Serve hot with plenty of maple syrup.

SAUTÉED APPLES

Ingredients:

- 2 tablespoons unsalted butter
- 2 large Golden Delicious apples (about 1 pound), peeled and sliced
- ½ cup raisins
- ½ teaspoon cinnamon
- ¼ cup maple syrup

Instructions:

- Melt the butter in a medium nonstick skillet over medium-high heat. When the butter foams, add the apple slices and sauté for 5 minutes or until tender. Add the raisins, cinnamon and maple syrup and cook for 1 more minute. Remove from heat and cool.

BANANA CRUMB MUFFINS

makes 6 large or 12 small muffins

Ingredients:

- ½ cup all-purpose flour
- ¼ cup granulated sugar
- 4 tablespoons unsalted butter, chilled, and cut into small pieces
- 2 teaspoons ground nutmeg
- 2 large eggs
- ½ cup light brown sugar
- 1 teaspoon vanilla extract
- 1 cup vegetable oil
- 3 large ripe bananas, mashed (about 1¼ cups)
- 2 cups whole-wheat pastry flour (available at health food stores or large supermarkets) or 1 cup cake flour and 1 cup whole-wheat flour
- 1½ teaspoons baking powder
- ½ teaspoon salt
- 1 cup coarsely chopped walnuts

Instructions:

- To make the streusel topping, combine the first 3 ingredients with ½ teaspoon of the nutmeg (save the remaining 1½ teaspoons for the muffin batter) in a medium mixing bowl. Knead the mixture with your hands until crumbly. Set aside.
- Preheat oven to 375°F. For large muffins, mist a 6-cup muffin tin with vegetable oil spray. For smaller muffins, mist a 12-cup muffin tin.
- In a medium mixing bowl, combine the eggs, brown sugar and vanilla. Add the oil and whisk until well incorporated. Stir in the bananas.
- In a separate large mixing bowl, combine the flour, baking powder, salt and the remaining nutmeg. Gently fold the flour mixture and nuts into the

banana mixture. Mix ingredients just until blended; too much mixing will make the muffins rise irregularly.
- Fill each muffin cup in the prepared tin ⅔ full of batter. Sprinkle tops with the streusel mixture.
- Bake large muffins for 20 to 24 minutes or until a toothpick inserted into the center of one comes out clean. Bake smaller muffins for 16 to 20 minutes. Transfer to a wire rack and cool slightly before serving. The muffins, sealed in an airtight container, may be frozen for 2 weeks. Defrost them overnight and warm them in a low oven before serving.

· **GOOD TO KNOW** ·

Christmas morning is special and you will want every detail to be perfect. A beautiful and quick way to serve your butter for these delicious muffins is to slide an 8-ounce tub of butter into a 1-pint Salt™ Crock! It fits perfectly and looks beautiful, too!

CITRUS BOWL with VANILLA YOGURT SAUCE

serves 6

Ingredients:

- 2 large navel oranges
- 2 blood oranges
- 1 white grapefruit
- 1 pink grapefruit
- 1 ruby red grapefruit
- 2 kiwis

Instructions:

- Cut the rind and white pith from the oranges and grapefruits. Cut between the individual membranes to release each citrus segment. Place in a nonreactive bowl. Peel the kiwis and slice into chunks.
- Gently toss the fruit together. Cover and refrigerate for up to 24 hours in advance.
- Serve with generous spoonfuls of Vanilla Yogurt Sauce.

VANILLA YOGURT SAUCE

Ingredients:

- 1 cup vanilla yogurt
- 1 teaspoon vanilla extract
- 1 tablespoon honey

Instructions:

- Mix all ingredients together in a sealable container and refrigerate for up to one week.

Christmas with the · Longabergers ·

Our founder, Dave Longaberger, grew up in a one-bath-room home with eleven siblings and his parents, J.W. and Bonnie Longaberger. In the days leading up to Christmas, not a single ornament or candy cane was in sight. When the kids woke on December 25th, they found that Christmas had come to their home overnight. To prolong the suspense, the little Longabergers waited on the stairs until the grownups gave the okay to come down to see the tree and the surprises beneath it. Today, our Longaberger Sales Consultants all across America tell us that their kids' same sense of wonder and suspense is their favorite part of the holiday season. Isn't it nice to know that some things never change?

· GOOD TO KNOW ·

If you'll be waking up bright and early Christmas morning to the pitter-patter of little feet scurrying to the tree, you'll probably need more than shrieks of joy to jolt you awake. If you don't want to miss the happy bedlam, be sure to program the coffeemaker the night before, and prep a Small Serving Tray with mugs and coasters placed in a Tarragon™ Basket.

· Christmas ·
At Longaberger

If you ever find yourself searching for the spirit of Christmas, come to Longaberger. You'll find it here in the crisp winter air, and in the heavenly voices of our employee choir. You'll find it in the thousands and thousands of white Christmas lights, traditional holiday trimmings and a basket-trimmed tree soaring three and a half stories high. At Longaberger, we believe.

•BRRR! HOORAY!•
SnowDay!

LAUGH OFF A WINTRY DAY WITH A PARTY
THAT MAKES TOTAL FUN OF IT.

When there's a foot of snow on the ground and a trip to Bermuda is out of the question, boost everyone's spirits with a party that celebrates winter. Everything on this party's menu can be purchased before the first snowflake falls, and the entertainment is as close as the nearest sledding hill or skating rink. No snow where you live? Turn up the A/C and pretend it's snowing outside!

· recipes ·

PANTRY CHILI
VEGETARIAN CHILI
COZY CORNBREAD
OATMEAL APPLE TOFFEE DROPS
CRYSTAL SNOWBALL COOKIES
OLD-FASHIONED HOT COCOA

· projects ·

SNOW DAY INVITATIONS
MARSHMALLOW SNOWMEN
SOCKED-IN SNOW FRIENDS

• getting started •

- It's easy to have fun in snow and on ice, but even easier to forget basic rules of safety.

- **In general:**

  Dress in several, lightweight layers.

  Wear mittens instead of gloves.

  Wear slip-proof boots that allow plenty of toe-wiggle room.

  Remove drawstrings from clothing.

  Put sunscreen on exposed skin, even if it's cloudy.

• TO DO LIST •

- **Before the snow falls:**

  Bleach "orphaned" white socks and stash them in a bag marked "Snow Day!"

  Stock up on project supplies.

  Stock up on menu ingredients.

  Make and freeze cookies.

- **Snow Day:**

  Enlist the kids' help to make and distribute invitations.

  Make chili.

  Make Cozy Cornbread.

  Defrost cookies.

  Make Old-Fashioned Hot Cocoa.

SNOW DAY INVITATIONS

SUPPLIES

Red construction paper
Plain white paper
Red marker
Hole punch
Large snowflake hole punch
Scissors

for each invitation:
24 inches of white yarn
Two large white pom-poms

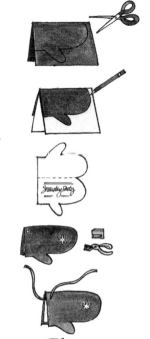

1. Fold a piece of red construction paper to your selected size. Cut out a mitten shape, keeping the fold intact.

2. Trace your red mitten onto a similarly folded piece of white paper. Cut out the white mitten about ⅛ inch inside of the trace line, so it is slightly smaller.

3. Use the red marker to write your party information on the inside lower half of the white mitten.

4. With the white mitten inside the red mitten, use the paper punch to make a round hole in the folded corner. Use the large snowflake punch to cut a snowflake in the center of the top red mitten only.

5. Thread 24 inches of white yarn through the round holes.

6. Attach pom-poms with a simple knot.

makes 12 snowmen

Instructions:

1. Cut the florist foam to fit inside the basket so that it is about 1½ inches below the basket's rim. Wrap the florist foam in wax paper or plastic wrap and fit inside the basket with protector. Mound with cotton balls to look like snow. Set aside.

2. Pour white candy sprinkles into a wide, shallow pan. Set aside.

3. Simmer white coating chips in the top of a double boiler, stirring occasionally until melted.

4. Thread 3 marshmallows onto each lollipop stick, leaving ¼ inch of lollipop stick peaking above the top marshmallow.

5. Hold the marshmallow sticks over the pan of melted coating chips and spoon the coating over the marshmallows. Quickly roll them in the white sprinkles.

6. Insert the coated marshmallow sticks into the florist foam and let cool.

To decorate:

1. To make hats, use a skewer or the end of a sharp knife to punch a hole into the middle of each chocolate wafer so that it can be threaded onto the top of the lollipop stick. This is the brim of the hat. Spoon a small dollop of white Royal Icing onto the top of the chocolate wafer, then place a chocolate kiss on top of the icing.

2. Use the white Royal Icing to "glue" on mini chocolate morsels for buttons and eyes. Add Tic Tacs for noses.

3. Use colored Royal Icing to pipe on smiles, holly sprigs, earmuffs—or whatever you can dream up!

SUPPLIES

12 ounces white coating chips ("candy melts")

36 large marshmallows

Twelve 8-inch lollipop sticks

1 cup white sprinkles

12 chocolate wafer cookies

12 Hershey's Chocolate Kisses - wrappers removed

1/4 cup mini chocolate morsels

24 pretzel sticks

1 pack orange Tic Tacs

1 package string red licorice

Green florist foam

Wax paper

1 recipe Royal Icing

Round basket, such as a Longaberger Darning Basket

Jumbo bag of cotton balls

4. Tie on a licorice string for a scarf.

5. Poke a pretzel stick into each side for arms.

ROYAL ICING

- 1 large egg white
- 1½ cups confectioners' sugar
- Red food coloring
- Green food coloring
- 3 zippered plastic bags

1. Beat the egg white with the confectioners' sugar until stiff. If the icing seems too thick add 1 or 2 drops of water. If too thin, add a few more tablespoons of confectioners' sugar.

2. Divide icing in half. One half will remain white. Divide the remaining half into two parts. Add red food coloring to one part and green food coloring to the other.

3. Put each color of icing into its own zippered plastic bag. Carefully cut a small opening across one corner of each bag. Squeeze icing out of corners.

• Come In from the Cold •

Have tissues at the ready when everyone comes in, and give each guest the luxury of a lip balm all their own. Buy a variety of fun flavors and personalize each one with a fine-tip permanent marker. Then let everyone have the fun of finding his or her own tube in a little basket like our Extra Small Gatehouse® Basket. Hang the basket either on a chair by the door, or beside the sink in the guest bathroom.

Station a basket beside the door and fill it with thick, cozy socks in a variety of sizes, ready for guests who come in with wet feet. What to do with all those snowy mittens, hats and scarves? Two ideas: One, tie a clothesline between two chairs and hang outdoor gear with clothespins. Or two, place an extra-large basket, like our Work-A-Round™ Basket, by the door to catch snowy clothes. The plastic protector keeps the basket's interior dry and prevents clothes from snagging. Throw the wet clothes in the dryer and when they're dry, make a game of sorting them. Start by throwing the dry clothes back in the basket. Then one at a time, blind-fold each participant and time how long each takes to find his or her outerwear and put it on. Now that's entertainment!

SUPPLIES

1 white sock for each

12 inches of elastic cording for each

One 20-ounce bag of navy beans or rice

White heavy-duty thread and needle

Twig branches for arms

Acrylic paint: ivory, black, orange and pink

Fine-point brush

Scissors

Glue

Novelty trims such as wooden buttons, mini straw hats, mini evergreen garland, rick rack, yarn or scraps of wintry fabrics for scarves and aprons

Transform ordinary white socks into these adorable Snow Day decorations or party favors. The bodies are easy to make, but a bit time-consuming, so assemble them beforehand and let guests have fun giving their snow friends faces and accessories.

1. Fill the foot portion of the sock with navy beans or rice. Tie off the top just below the cuff with a few good wraps and secure with elastic cording. Snip off ends of cording. With another piece of elastic cording, tie again at the neck, about halfway down.

2. Start creating your snow friend by sewing or gluing on buttons, making hats, scarves, etc.

3. Paint an ivory circle where you would like the face to be. Use a fine-point brush to blush in cheeks, dot in eyes and mouth, and brush in a carrot nose.

4. Stitch on twig branches for arms. Say hello to your new snow friend!

• Snow Day Memories •

You might think it odd that two of the Longaberger children have the same favorite memory of snow days here in Ohio. Then again, if you knew their grandfather, company founder Dave Longaberger (whom they called "Pop-Pop") maybe it's not so unexpected.

Rachel Longaberger's son Dustin says, "When school gets called off because of snow, I think, 'Yes! No homework!' Then I'll roll over and go back to sleep. When I get up I'll probably talk online with some friends. Maybe later we'll all get together to play outside. The best time I ever had playing in the snow was with Pop-Pop. Sledding at his house was so much fun."

Dustin's cousin, Tami Longaberger's daughter Claire, agrees. "When we have a snow day, the first thing I want to do is go sledding. One time my friend and I spent the whole day sledding and playing outside at my grandpa's house. It was always fun to go to his house, because he would play jokes on us kids."

• GOOD IDEA •

A few simple decorations can make this snowy get-together a memorable one. Have scissors and white paper on hand and let kids have a ball making all sizes of paper snowflakes, which you can then use to decorate the party area. Use a snowflake paper punch to turn paper scraps into a drift of confetti to sprinkle across party tables.

• recipes •

PANTRY CHILI

serves 10

Ingredients:
- 2 pounds ground chuck
- Four 15.5-ounce cans tomato sauce
- Two 15.5-ounce cans chili seasoning sauce
- Two 15.5-ounce cans kidney beans, rinsed and drained
- Two 1.25-ounce packages chili seasoning (regular, mild or hot)
- Variety of chopped fresh chilies, optional (see Variations)

Instructions:
- Over medium-high heat brown the ground chuck in a large, heavy-bottomed pan, such as a Dutch oven or a deep skillet. Drain in a colander.
- Return the meat to the pan, add all the remaining ingredients and bring to a boil over medium heat, stirring frequently. Reduce the heat to low and simmer 60 minutes or until the chili is thick, stirring regularly. (You can also cook the chili in a crockpot. Use a skillet to brown the meat, and then add the drained meat to the crockpot with the remaining ingredients. Cook on low for 6 hours.)
- Serve alongside bowls of sour cream, chopped scallions, shredded cheddar cheese, and any optional chopped chilies.

• Serving • Suggestion

Adult-size portions can overwhelm little guests. For chili servings that are just the right size for kids, try using our Woven Traditions® Small Dessert Bowls.

• VARIATIONS •

HEAT IT UP

Not everyone likes spicy food, so we suggest serving a mild version of chili, accompanied by a variety of fresh, chopped chilies served separately to accommodate guests who like their chili spicier. Remember, you can turn up the heat by adding more of one kind of chili, or by adding hotter varieties of chilies.

Wear gloves when chopping chilies. Soap and water are only partially effective in removing irritating chili oils, so avoid contact with eyes and areas of sensitive skin even after you've washed your hands thoroughly.

Most of a chili's heat is found in the seeds and in the ribs that hold the seeds, so discard the seeds and scrape off the white ribs inside.

Label bowls of chilies so guests know exactly what they're getting!
Mild - Poblano peppers
Medium - Jalapeno peppers
Hot - Serrano peppers
Wild - Habanero peppers or Scotch bonnets

COOL IT DOWN

To tone down too-spicy chili, try squeezing some fresh lime juice on it, or adding a generous dollop of sour cream.

VEGETARIAN CHILI

serves 10 *to* 12

Ingredients:

- ¼ cup vegetable oil
- 2 large onions, diced (about 3 cups)
- 2 red peppers, cored, seeded and diced (about 2 cups)
- 4 cloves garlic, minced
- 2 tablespoons ground cumin
- 2 teaspoons ground coriander
- 1 teaspoon cayenne pepper
- 2 teaspoons paprika
- 3 tablespoons chili powder
- 1 tablespoon dried oregano
- 2 teaspoons salt
- 1 teaspoon freshly cracked black pepper
- Two 28-ounce cans diced tomatoes, drained
- One 28-ounce can crushed tomatoes
- One 16-ounce jar medium-hot salsa
- 12 ounces beer
- Two 15.5-ounce cans white hominy, drained
- Two 15.5-ounce cans black beans, drained
- Two 15.5-ounce cans kidney beans, drained
- Two 4-ounce cans diced green chilies
- Juice of 2 limes
- One 8-ounce bag frozen corn
- 1 bunch fresh cilantro, stems removed, coarsely chopped

Instructions:

- Heat the oil in a heavy-bottom, 8-quart (or larger) pot over medium-high heat. Add the onions, peppers and garlic and cook for 5 minutes, stirring frequently, until the vegetables are soft.
- Combine the 8 spices and seasonings in a small bowl, and then add the mixture to the vegetables. Cook for an additional 5 minutes, stirring frequently.
- Add the tomatoes, salsa and beer. Lower the heat to medium and simmer for 15 minutes. Add the hominy, beans, chilies and lime juice and simmer for 30 to 40 minutes.
- Stir in the corn, heating it thoroughly for 5 to 7 minutes. Mix in the fresh cilantro and serve the chili accompanied by white rice, grated cheddar cheese, chopped scallions, sour cream and lime wedges.

COZY CORNBREAD

makes one 9x13-inch pan or 24 medium-size muffins

Ingredients:
- 3 cups yellow cornmeal
- 1¼ cups all-purpose flour
- 4 teaspoons baking powder
- 2 teaspoons baking soda
- 1½ teaspoons salt
- 2 tablespoons granulated sugar
- 2½ cups buttermilk
- 3 large eggs, lightly beaten
- 6 tablespoons vegetable oil
- 6 tablespoons unsalted butter, melted

Instructions:
- Preheat oven to 425°F. Lightly mist a 9x13-inch baking pan with vegetable oil.
- Combine the cornmeal, flour, baking powder, baking soda, salt and sugar in a large mixing bowl. In another mixing bowl, whisk together the buttermilk, eggs, oil and butter. Pour the wet ingredients into the dry ingredients and fold together just until blended.
- Pour batter into the prepared pan and bake 25 to 28 minutes, or until a toothpick inserted into the center of the cornbread comes out clean.
- Cool for 5 minutes before cutting cornbread into squares. It's best served warm.

· GOOD IDEA ·

Measure the cornbread dry ingredients into a 1-quart jar. Close tightly and store in your pantry until you're ready to mix up some warm, homemade cornbread for a Snow Day party or for a cold winter night's chili supper.

· VARIATIONS ·

Cornbread Additions:

Blueberry Corn Muffins: Fold 2 cups fresh blueberries into the batter.

Cheddar Cornbread: Fold in 1 cup sharp cheddar cheese.

Hot Cornbread: Add 1/4 cup chopped canned green chilies

Double-Corn Cornbread: Add 1 cup fresh corn kernels.

Mexican Cornbread: Add 1 tablespoon chili powder.

Maximum Cornbread: Add the cheese, chilies, corn and chili powder. Allow a few extra minutes baking time.

OATMEAL APPLE TOFFEE DROPS

makes 9 dozen 2¼ inch cookies

Ingredients:

- 1 cup (2 sticks) unsalted butter, softened
- ½ cup granulated sugar
- ½ cup light brown sugar
- 2 large eggs
- 1 tablespoon dark rum or 2 teaspoons vanilla extract
- 1½ cups all-purpose flour
- 2 teaspoons apple-pie or pumpkin-pie spice
- ½ teaspoon baking powder
- ¼ teaspoon baking soda
- ¼ teaspoon salt
- 2 cups old-fashioned oats
- One 10-ounce package English toffee bits
- 9 ounces dried apples, chopped

Instructions:

- Preheat oven to 350°F. Line 2 sheet pans with parchment paper or silicone mats.
- Cream the butter in the bowl of an electric mixer. Add the sugars and beat for 1 minute. Add the eggs and rum or vanilla extract and mix again until combined. Scrape the sides of the bowl.
- Combine the flour, spice, baking powder, baking soda and salt in a mixing bowl. Add the combined dry ingredients to the batter and mix until just blended. Add the oats, toffee bits and chopped dried apple. Mix for 30 seconds or until just combined.
- Drop the mixture by tablespoonfuls onto the lined pans, about 2 inches apart. Wet the palm of one hand with water and lightly flatten the tops of the cookies.
- Bake 8 to 10 minutes or until cookies are a light golden brown.
- Cool for 1 minute then transfer to cooling racks. Store in an airtight container for up to 1 week. Frozen, they keep for up to 3 months.

· GOOD TO KNOW ·

Maximize space and dress up your dessert buffet by utilizing our Wrought Iron Paper Tray Stand with WoodCrafts Shelves and Paper Tray Basket with 6-way divided protector. Serve a 16-ounce tub of whipped topping in a Button Basket for a delicious presentation.

OLD-FASHIONED HOT COCOA

serves 6-8

Ingredients:
- 4 cups whole milk
- 2 cups half-and-half
- ½ cup malted milk powder (plain or chocolate)
- 1½ cups hot fudge sauce
- 2 teaspoons vanilla extract
- Optional garnishes: whipped cream, marshmallows, marshmallow fluff, cinnamon sticks, peppermint sticks, chocolate curls

Instructions:
- Combine the first four ingredients in a large, heavy-bottomed saucepan. Place the pan over medium-high heat and bring to a simmer, whisking constantly. Stir in the vanilla. Serve in mugs or pour cocoa into a thermal carafe to keep warm. Serve with optional garnishes.

CRYSTAL SNOWBALL COOKIES

makes 3 *dozen*

Ingredients:
- 1 cup (2 sticks) unsalted butter
- ½ cup granulated sugar
- Pinch of salt
- 1 teaspoon pure vanilla extract
- 2 cups all-purpose flour
- ¾ cup finely chopped pecans
- Confectioners' sugar
- Edible white glitter, optional (available at cake decorating centers)

Instructions:
- Preheat oven to 350°F. Line 2 baking sheets with parchment paper or silicone mats. Set aside.
- Cream the butter in the bowl of an electric mixer. Add the sugar and beat for 1 minute, or until fluffy. Add the salt and vanilla and mix for 30 seconds. Remove the bowl from the mixer and add the flour and nuts. Mix by hand with a wooden spoon until the dough just comes together.
- Shape the dough into small balls and place them 1 inch apart on the prepared baking sheets. Bake 8 to 12 minutes or until the bottoms and the edges of the cookies begin to turn light brown.
- Cool the cookies on the baking sheets for 5 minutes. Place the confectioners' sugar in a medium bowl. When the cookies are cool enough to handle, roll them in the sugar and transfer them to a cooling rack. For slightly sweeter cookies, roll again in confectioners' sugar. If you'd like, dust the finished cookies with the edible glitter.
- The cookies will keep 2 weeks in an airtight container, or up to 3 months in the freezer.

SPRING

Spring in the heart of Ohio always comes as a surprise. We go to bed one night in the cold and dark of winter and wake up the next morning to daffodils and robins' songs. We celebrate by gathering our favorite people around us at Easter, making kid-catered breakfasts on Mother's Day, and showering brides-to-be with pretty flowers and good wishes. So forget about spring cleaning—let's start spring partying!

· EASTER · Joy

CELEBRATE THE WONDER OF SPRING WITH A LEISURELY DINNER
AT A TABLE SURROUNDED BY THE PEOPLE YOU LOVE MOST.

Easter Sunday should be as joyous an occasion for the hostess as it is for the guests. That's why you'll find this celebration simple to plan, and simple to pull off, with just enough special touches to flaunt your creative flair. The just-this-side-of-traditional menu is designed to please all ages—with plenty of room left for dessert. You'll find fun ideas for keeping the kids occupied, and quick tips for streamlining the to-do list even further. All of which leaves you with more time to do what you do best: Organize the egg hunt!

· recipes ·

GLAZED HAM *with* MUSTARD SAUCE
CARROTS AND SUGAR SNAP PEAS *in* CHIVE BUTTER
AU GRATIN POTATOES
SPRING SALAD *with* SHERRY VINAIGRETTE
LITTLE CHICKIE PUDDING CUPS
ALMOND CREAM CAKE *with* FRESH PINEAPPLE SAUCE

· projects ·

VOTIVE CUP PLACE CARDS
LITTLE CHICKIE PLACE CARDS
FUN NAPKIN FOLDS

· getting started ·

· PLANNING TIPS ·

- Plan a few activities to keep excited kids calm while you wait for other guests to arrive. Try hopscotch, jacks and tic-tac-toe. Use jellybeans!

- Set an extra spot for Grandpa at the kids' table. He'll probably end up there anyway!

- Use a treat-filled Easter basket to serve as the kids' table centerpiece. Set their table with kid-size dinnerware, like our luncheon plates, salad forks and 12-ounce tumblers.

- Plant a few promises of future family fun in with the treats for the egg hunt, like coupons good for an afternoon bike ride or a family trip to a water park when warmer weather arrives.

· TO DO LIST ·

- **1-2 Weeks Before:**
  Decorate eggs for hunts and decorations (not eating).
  Prepare Mustard Sauce and refrigerate.
  Make Little Chickie Place Cards.
  Make Little Chickie pudding toppers; store in airtight container.

- **Day Before:**
  Prepare Sherry Vinaigrette and refrigerate.
  Prepare Almond Cream Cake and Pineapple Sauce.
  Prepare Au Gratin Potatoes and refrigerate.
  Fold napkins and set tables.

- **Party Day:**
  Assemble Votive Cup Place Cards.
  Prepare Carrots and Sugar Snap Peas in Chive Butter.
  Prepare Glazed Ham.
  Prepare Spring Salad. Toss with Sherry Vinaigrette just before serving.
  Prepare pudding and assemble Little Chickie Pudding Cups.

VOTIVE CUP PLACE CARDS

SUPPLIES
for each:

Longaberger Votive Cup
Decorated Easter egg
1-1/2-inch square
of wheat grass sod
Construction paper
White paper
Glue stick
Pen

1. Make a simple place card by folding a 1½x3-inch piece of construction paper in half. Center and glue on a 1¼-inch square of coordinating paper. Then glue on a 1-inch square of white paper creating an even border. Fill in your guest's name with a pen, keeping the fold at the top.

2. The day of the party, cut the wheat grass sod into 1½-inch squares. Wheat grass sod is available in health food stores and local home and garden centers. Nestle the grass into the Votive Cup. Top with a beautifully decorated Easter egg.

3. Position the place card next to the votive as shown.

· EGGCEPTIONAL SAFETY ·

Did you know that most commercial egg producers lightly mist their eggs with mineral oil to close the pores against contamination? Cooking the eggs in their shells removes that protective barrier, exposing them to contamination. If you intend to eat your eggs after decorating and hiding them, remember:

1. Cook the eggs until both the white and the yolk are completely firm.
2. Don't hide eggs in places where they might come in contact with animals, birds, reptiles, insects or lawn chemicals.
3. If you won't be coloring your eggs right after cooking them, store them in their cartons in the refrigerator.
4. Promptly refrigerate eggs after the Easter egg hunt.
5. Don't eat cracked eggs, or eggs that have been out of refrigeration for more than two hours.
6. Since the eggs in our Votive Cup Place Cards will be left out for more than a few hours, please don't eat them.

SUPPLIES

for each Chick:

Fluffy yellow yarn

3x4-inch piece of cardboard

1 sheet orange craft foam

Black & white paper

Large & small hole punch

Scissors

Glue stick

for each Place Card:

3x3/4-inch strip of construction paper

2-3/4x1/2-inch strip of white paper

Glue stick

Pen

1. Wrap the yarn about 100 times around the cardboard. Tie each side through the middle with a small strand of yarn.

2. Cut through the top edges, then through the bottom edges. Tie both bundles together.

3. Fluff and trim into an oval "chick" shape.

4. Cut a tiny beak and funny feet out of the craft foam and glue into place.

5. Make eyes from large white punched holes and small black punched holes and glue into place.

6. For the place card, glue the thin strip of white paper onto the wider construction paper strip. Add the guest's name with a pen and place in front of the chick.

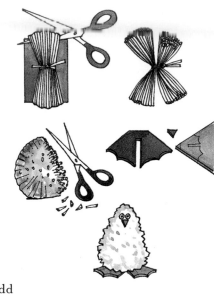

Madeline

• The Thrill of the Hunt •

Finding Easter eggs is fun, and finding them with surprises inside is even more exciting. Big bags of plastic eggs are inexpensive, you can buy tons, and if you'll be hiding them outside the night before, plastic is your best option for protecting the contents from sudden spring rains. Fill them with small candies and coins. Tuck in a few coupons good for bigger surprises, too, like a new kite or a future trip to the ice-cream store. And don't forget that every participant will need a loot-gathering basket!

FAN NAPKIN FOLD

1. Start with a square fabric napkin folded in half lengthwise.

2. Pleat the napkin at about 1-inch intervals.

3. Secure pleats near the bottom with a ribbon bow.

4. Fan the pleats and place the ribboned end in a glass tumbler.

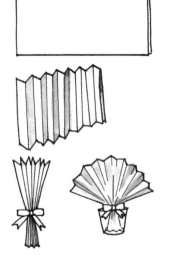

BOAT NAPKIN FOLD

1. Start with a square fabric napkin folded into a smaller square.

2. Fold the top two corners into the center to create a point.

3. Fold the bottom edges up toward the point once.

4. Fold the bottom up one more time and secure the ends with tape, if desired.

5. Fluff into a boat shape.

· GOOD TO KNOW ·

Nothing lights up a room like pots of fresh spring flowers in full bloom. Chances are you can pick up a few pots in the floral department of your grocery store, right along with your Easter dinner groceries. When you get home, just slip those 4-inch pots of daffodils and crocus right into our 1-quart Utensil™ Crocks. If you're feeling ambitious, you can force your own flower bulbs in pots. Look for pre-chilled bulbs at nurseries or order them online. Plant your bulbs according to the grower's instructions. Give them a turn now and then to keep them from leaning towards the sun. Schedule your forcing start date with the grower's instructions in mind so that you'll have peak blooms on Easter morning.

GLAZED HAM WITH MUSTARD SAUCE

serves 8 *to* 10

Ingredients:
- One 8- to 9-pound ham
  (bone-in, fully cooked spiral ham)

Glaze Ingredients:
- ¼ cup bourbon
- 1 cup light brown sugar
- ½ cup whole-grain mustard
- ½ cup pure maple syrup
- Zest of 1 orange
- ¼ cup fresh orange juice

Instructions:
- Preheat oven to 300°F. Position the racks to allow room for the ham on the lowest rack.
- Place the ham in a large roasting pan. Combine the glaze ingredients in a medium mixing bowl and spoon the glaze over the entire ham. Cover loosely with aluminum foil and bake 30 minutes. Remove the foil and baste the ham with the glaze every 15 minutes for an additional 45 to 60 minutes. (Fully cooked hams need 10 to 12 minutes per pound to reach an internal temperature of 140°F.)
- Remove ham from the oven and raise the oven temperature to 425°F. Pour most of the cooking juices into a small bowl. Spoon some of the juices over the ham, then return to the oven for 5 to 8 minutes, or until the ham is golden brown.
- Transfer the ham to a platter. Loosely cover it with foil and let set for 10 minutes before serving. Serve with Mustard Sauce.

MUSTARD SAUCE

Ingredients:
- ½ cup mustard
- 3 tablespoons pure maple syrup
- Freshly cracked black pepper, to taste

Instructions:
- Combine all the ingredients in an airtight container. Shake vigorously. The sauce will keep for several weeks in the refrigerator.

· GOOD IDEA ·

On a particularly busy day, you can easily prepare a ham for dinner: Wrap a fully cooked boneless ham in foil and cook it in a slow cooker on low, with the lid on, for 4-6 hours. It will be moist and delicious with little effort on your part.

CARROTS AND SUGAR SNAP PEAS IN CHIVE BUTTER

serves 6

Ingredients:
- 1½ pounds carrots (7 to 8 medium carrots), peeled and cut diagonally into ½-inch slices
- 8 ounces fresh sugar snap peas (about 2 cups)
- ½ cup chicken or vegetable stock
- 2 tablespoons unsalted butter
- ¼ cup chopped fresh parsley
- ¼ cup chopped fresh chives
- Salt and freshly ground black pepper

Instructions:
- Bring 2 medium pots of water to a boil.
- Cook the sliced carrots in one pot for 3 to 5 minutes, or until tender. Drain and rinse the carrots with cold water.
- Cook the peas in the second pot for 1 minute. Drain and rinse with cold water.
- Pour the stock into a large skillet and bring to a boil over medium-high heat. Add the carrots and peas and cook for 3 to 5 minutes, or until the stock has reduced by half. Add the butter, parsley, and chives and stir gently. Season with salt and pepper, toss briefly and serve.

We're in · Daffodil Heaven ·

After a long midwestern winter, all of us at Longaberger are ready to welcome spring in a big way. That's why, from our tiny hometown of Dresden, Ohio to our Home Office in Newark (shown here), and all along the miles of white picket fence in between, we brighten up every spring with more than 74,000 daffodils!

serves 6

Ingredients:

- 2 cups chicken stock
- 2 tablespoons unsalted butter, plus extra for pan
- 1 large onion, sliced (2 cups)
- 2 large garlic cloves cut into slivers
- 2½ pounds Russet potatoes (3 jumbo or 6 medium)
- 2 teaspoons fresh thyme leaves or 1 teaspoon dried thyme
- 1 teaspoon paprika, optional
- Salt and freshly ground pepper
- 2 tablespoons all-purpose flour
- ½ cup whole milk
- 4 ounces Gruyere cheese, grated (about 1½ cups)
- ½ cup grated Parmesan cheese

Instructions:

- Preheat oven to 375°F. Butter a 9-inch pie plate.
- Heat 1 cup of stock and the butter in a large skillet over medium heat. Add the onion and garlic, bring to a boil, and cook until all of the liquid has evaporated. Continue to sauté the onions until they caramelize, about 3 to 5 minutes, stirring frequently. Transfer the onions to a large mixing bowl.
- Peel the potatoes and slice into ¼-inch rounds, using a sharp knife, food processor outfitted with a slicing disk, or a mandoline. Work quickly to keep the potatoes from oxidizing. Add the slices to the cooled onions, sprinkle with thyme, optional paprika, salt, pepper and flour, and gently toss together.

- Add the milk, remaining cup of stock, and half of the Gruyere cheese. Combine well and pour the mixture into the prepared pie plate. Sprinkle with the remaining Gruyere, followed by the Parmesan.
- Cover loosely with foil; place the pie plate on a baking sheet on the middle shelf of the oven and bake for 1 hour.
- Raise the temperature to 400°F, remove the foil and bake for an additional 30 to 40 minutes or until the potatoes are tender when poked with a knife and the cheeses are golden brown. If the top browns too quickly, cover again with foil until the potatoes are fully cooked.
- Allow to set for 10 minutes before serving.

Completely cooled and tightly covered, the potatoes may be refrigerated 1 day in advance. To reheat, remove the dish from the refrigerator 30 minutes prior to reheating. Cover the dish with parchment paper and then aluminum foil. Bake at 300°F for 35 to 45 minutes or until hot.

> **· GOOD IDEA ·**
>
> AFTER-EASTER TREATS
>
> Save your Easter dinner ham bone to make pea, navy bean or lentil soup. Slice and freeze meal-size portions of ham to use later in scalloped potatoes, or dice and freeze the ham to toss into next week's scrambled eggs. If you have an excess of chocolate bunnies, chop them coarsely and make chocolate-chunk cookie dough. Freeze the dough in rolls, then slice and bake it once the Easter Bunny's treats have all been gobbled up.

serves 6

Ingredients:

- 2 large heads Belgian endive
- 1 large head Boston or Bibb lettuce
- 1 bunch watercress, large stems removed
- 1 recipe Sherry Vinaigrette
- 3 oranges, peeled and sectioned or sliced
- ½ cup toasted or candied walnuts
- 4 ounces mild goat cheese, crumbled

Instructions:

- Remove any blemished or wilted outer leaves on the endive. Slice off the base of the endive and separate individual leaves.
- Wrap 18 of the largest leaves in damp paper towels. Slice the remaining leaves into ½-inch pieces.
- Remove any wilted outer leaves on the Bibb lettuce. Select 6 leaves and wrap these in damp paper towels. Chop the remaining leaves into 1-inch square pieces.
- In a large mixing bowl, combine both chopped lettuces with the watercress. Drizzle with 2 tablespoons of the Sherry Vinaigrette and toss well.
- Arrange dressed greens on 6 chilled salad plates as follows: Place 3 whole endive leaves in a triangle. Place 1 whole Bibb leaf in the center. Spoon a portion of the dressed greens in the center of each Bibb lettuce "cup." Sprinkle with nuts and cheese. Top each salad with several orange sections and drizzle with Sherry Vinaigrette.

SHERRY VINAIGRETTE

makes ¾ cup

Ingredients:

- 3 tablespoons sherry vinegar (available at specialty food stores and larger supermarkets)
- 1 large shallot, minced (2 tablespoons)
- 1 teaspoon fresh thyme leaves, minced or ¼ teaspoon dried thyme
- 1 teaspoon sugar
- 2 teaspoons Dijon mustard
- ½ cup extra-virgin olive oil
- Salt and freshly cracked black pepper

Instructions:

- Combine the first 5 ingredients in a mixing bowl. Add the oil in a slow stream, whisking continuously until the dressing emulsifies. Season with salt and pepper, to taste. The dressing may be prepared 2 to 3 days in advance and refrigerated in an airtight container. Shake or whisk just before serving.

· VARIATION ·

For an attractive alternative, substitute chopped pears or apples for the oranges; instead of the goat cheese, try a tangy blue cheese.

makes 2-3 dozen decorations

Ingredients:

- 1 pound ready-to-use white rolled fondant (a simple sugar-water-cream of tartar mixture cooked to the soft-ball stage), available in cake decorating stores
- 1-2 drops clear vanilla or favorite extract flavor
- Food coloring paste, available in cake decorating stores
- Cornstarch, for work surface
- Prepared pudding, flavor of your choice
- Chick cookie cutter

Instructions:

- To flavor the fondant, knead in a few drops of your favorite extract. Taste to make sure it is evenly distributed and has enough flavor.
- Next, divide the fondant into 2 or more pieces (if making the chicks in the grass, like in the photo, you will need 1 ounce of white for the eyes and the remaining 15 ounces can be evenly divided for the chicks and the grass). Add very small amounts of food coloring paste to create favorite pastel colors. Knead the color all the way through before adding more. Wrap each piece in plastic wrap.

- Lightly dust work surface with cornstarch and roll out the fondant to about ⅛ inch thick. Using a small chick cookie cutter, cut out as many chicks as possible. Remove all excess fondant around the chicks, save and re-roll for more chicks.
- Carefully transfer the chicks with a spatula to a tray lined with wax or parchment paper.
- To add an eye, roll out the white fondant. Using the small opening at the end of a pastry tip, cut out small dots. Dampen the backside of the eye with a small droplet of water and place on the chick. Allow chicks to dry for one day, uncovered, then place in an air-tight container until ready to use. The decorations can be made up to 2 weeks in advance.
- To create grass, press small amounts of green fondant through a garlic press onto a tray lined with wax or parchment paper. Use a small paring knife to release the strands of grass. Dry and store the decoration as listed above.
- At serving time, fill mugs with pudding, top with a small bundle of grass, add a chick and serve.

• What's Easter • Without Baskets?

Can you imagine gathering colored eggs, jellybeans and chocolate bunnies in plastic bags or cardboard boxes? We can't either. In fact, we bet no one loves Easter more than Longaberger, because no one loves Easter baskets more than we do. Our baskets have been part of the Easter tradition since the days before our founder, Dave Longaberger, was born. His dad, J.W., would weave each of his twelve children a new Easter basket each year–big kids got big baskets and little ones received little baskets. Often J.W. would dye hardwood splints to match the colors of his family's Easter eggs. We continue J.W.'s tradition of making brand-new Easter basket designs each year, which we share with millions of families all across America. Leave it to us to make sure that beautiful baskets and Easter will always go together.

• VARIATION •

We used pudding for our chickie cups, but ice cream, gelatin or iced cupcakes work equally as well.

serves 12

Ingredients:
- One 18-ounce box yellow cake mix
- ½ cup finely ground almonds
- 3 large eggs
- 10 tablespoons unsalted butter, melted
- 8 ounces cream cheese
- 2 cups confectioners' sugar, plus extra for dusting
- 1 teaspoon pure almond extract
- ½ cup slivered almonds
- 1 recipe Fresh Pineapple Sauce
- Fresh mint sprigs, for garnish

Instructions:
- Preheat oven to 350°F. Lightly mist a 9x13-inch, nonreactive baking dish with vegetable oil spray.
- In a medium mixing bowl, combine the cake mix and ground almonds. In a small mixing bowl, whisk together 1 egg and the melted butter, then add it to the dry mix, stirring just until it forms a dough. Pat the dough evenly across the bottom of the prepared baking dish.
- In the bowl of an electric mixer, beat the cream cheese at medium speed for 1 minute or until smooth. Add the sugar and beat an additional minute. Scrape the sides of the bowl, add the 2 remaining eggs and the almond extract, and mix on low speed for 30 seconds. Scrape the sides of the bowl again and mix an addi-

tional 30 seconds until the batter is smooth.
- Pour the batter over the dough layer. Sprinkle with the almond slivers and bake for 30 to 35 minutes, or until the top layer is firm.
- Allow the cake to cool completely, then cover and refrigerate for up to 2 days before serving. Dust the cake with confectioners' sugar before slicing. Serve slices garnished with a spoonful of Fresh Pineapple Sauce topped with a fresh mint sprig.

FRESH PINEAPPLE SAUCE
makes 2 cups

Ingredients:
- 2 cups fresh pineapple, cut into 1- to 2-inch pieces
- 2 tablespoons dark rum or almond liqueur
- 1 tablespoon chopped fresh mint
- 1 to 2 tablespoons granulated sugar, optional

Instructions:
- Purée pineapple in a food processor; or for chunky sauce, purée half the pineapple and dice the rest.
- In a small bowl, combine the pineapple with the rum and chopped mint. Mix thoroughly and taste; depending upon the pineapple's sweetness, you may need to add up to 2 tablespoons of sugar.
- Sauce may be prepared 1 day in advance and refrigerated in an airtight container.

·MOM'S BIG· Day

IF YOU'RE A MOM, MARK THIS PAGE FOR DAD AND SKIP TO THE NEXT CELEBRATION IN THE BOOK! DADS AND KIDS, READ ON: HERE'S EVERYTHING YOU NEED TO MAKE THIS MOTHER'S DAY HER BEST EVER.

While the rest of the family is busy in the kitchen, give Mom the luxury of a late morning in bed. When she wakes up, take her a cup of hot coffee, a bowl of fresh berries and her Mother's Day gifts. Don't forget homemade cards, and either the morning newspaper or her favorite magazine. If you really want to impress her, make a show of raising the shades, plumping her pillows and turning on a little soft music. Before you tiptoe quietly out of the room, kiss her on the cheek and tell her she's the best.

· recipes ·

BACON BITES
SIMPLE SURPRISE PANCAKES
SWEET HEART TOAST
JAVA TWISTS

· projects ·

DECOUPAGE FRAME
PROMISE BOXES

10 More Ways · to Make Mom's · Day Great

1. Instead of a photo, draw a self-portrait for your Decoupage Frame (pg. 75).
2. Kids, clean your room! Dad, clean the garage!
3. Make her a pretty bookmark.
4. Give her one whole hour alone. No interruptions.
5. Ban loud music.
6. Go to a garden center with her and help her pick out flowers for the yard. Then help her plant them.
7. Go for a walk around the block, to the park or wherever she wants to go.
8. Give her one hug every hour on the hour. Set a timer.
9. Let her have control of the TV remote.
10. If she's far away, call her. Not collect.

PROMISE BOXES

SUPPLIES

Empty matchboxes
(a big one might be
best for Dad)
Wrapping paper
Construction paper
Ribbon
Writing paper
Pen or pencil
Scissors
Glue stick
Ruler
Hole punch

Promises are easy to make, and only a little harder to keep. Some promises your Mom might like are, "I promise to make my bed every day," or "I promise to call my mom once a week when I'm grown."

1. Measure and cut the wrapping paper to fit the matchbox. Glue the paper onto the box.

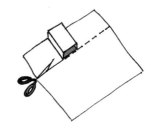

2. Cut and fold a little piece of writing paper to fit inside the matchbox tray.

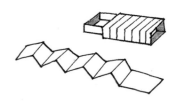

3. Write your promise (or promises) on the little piece of paper and slip it into the box.

4. Tie the box with a pretty bow. If you'd like, cut a simple flower shape out of construction paper, punch a hole in the center and pull the ribbon through the hole before tying the bow.

BACON BITES

Ingredients:
- Bacon
- Maple syrup
- Light brown sugar

Instructions:
- Preheat oven to 375°F. Line a baking sheet with aluminum foil.
- Cut any amount of bacon strips in half. Place bacon on foil and bake for 10 minutes, or until the bacon is half-cooked.
- Remove pan from the oven, pour off excess fat, and wipe the pouring side of the pan clean. Brush each piece of bacon with pure maple syrup, and sprinkle with 1 teaspoon of light brown sugar.
- Return pan to the oven and bake 12 to 15 minutes, or until bacon is browned and crisp. Drain bacon bites and allow to cool slightly before serving.

• recipes •

SIMPLE SURPRISE PANCAKES

What's so surprising about these pancakes? They're easy! Just follow the directions on your favorite box of pancake mix, or make your favorite basic pancake batter. Then look below and choose one or two of our simple suggestions for making your pancakes surprisingly delicious!

BATTER ADDITIONS:
- A few drops of vanilla extract
- Finely chopped orange or lemon zest
- A dash of cinnamon

GRIDDLE ADDITIONS; ADD BEFORE FLIPPING:
- Fresh blueberries
- Dried sour cherries
- Cranberries
- Toasted chopped pecans

TOPPINGS:
- A dollop of lemon curd and a sprinkling of fresh blueberries
- Diced bananas, chopped macadamia nuts and toasted coconut
- Fruit syrup with fresh berries
- Apple or pumpkin butter, toasted pecans and a dollop of sour cream

· GOOD TO KNOW ·

So everyone can join Mom at the breakfast table for pancakes, cook them ahead of time, and keep them warm in a 250°F oven until you're ready to sit down. Put short stacks on individual Woven Traditions® pottery plates, or pile the whole batch in a covered casserole or on a large platter. Because Woven Traditions pottery is vitrified, it can go from oven to table beautifully, retaining heat to keep foods warmer longer.

· GOOD IDEA ·

Use our pottery Votive Cups to create quick and pretty floral arrangements that will make Mom grin. Simply fill the Votive Cups with water and fresh flowers cut to fit. Place them throughout the house for a fresh, springtime accent.

SWEET HEART TOAST

Ingredients:
- ¼ cup confectioners' sugar
- 1 teaspoon ground cinnamon
- 4 pieces toasting bread
- Unsalted butter
- Heart-shaped cookie cutter

Instructions:
- Combine confectioners' sugar and cinnamon in a small bowl. Toast the bread to a golden brown and generously spread warm toast with butter. Sprinkle toast with 1 tablespoon of the cinnamon and sugar mixture. Let the mixture soak in for a few seconds, then spread it around evenly with a table knife. Use a heart-shaped cookie cutter to cut away the center of each toast.

Serve Sweet Heart Toast with:
- Assorted jams, jellies or marmalades
- Whipped butter
- Honey, maple or fruit butter
- Flavored cream cheese
- Honey
- Apple or pumpkin butter

JAVA TWISTS

Any of these additions to Mom's coffee will give it a delicious new twist:

- For a richly scented cup of coffee, stir in a few drops of pure vanilla extract.

- Make a chocoholic happy by drizzling in a few table-spoons of chocolate sauce.

- Warm 1 cup of skim milk and whisk vigorously to create a foam. Stir any amount of the foam into a cup of dark coffee, and top it off with another spoonful of foam. Finish with a dusting of cinnamon.

- A simple dollop of sweetened whipped cream turns a cup of rich, dark coffee into a luscious treat.

- Before brewing, add a few broken cinnamon sticks, 1 split and scraped vanilla bean, and 1 strip of orange peel to coffee grounds for an exotic, spicy pot of coffee.

· GOOD TO KNOW ·

We like to serve toast and pancake toppers in Woven Traditions® Votive Cups lined up in our Cracker Basket.

· Discover Longaberger ·

SPRING
Showers

HONOR THE BRIDE-TO-BE WITH LADYLIKE TEA SANDWICHES AND SCRUMPTIOUS
FRUIT TARTS, SERVED IN A GARDEN YOU CREATE WITH SIMPLE TISSUE PAPER.

There's a trend toward co-ed wedding showers these days, but we believe that fancy parties given by women for women will never go out of style. It's such fun to indulge in all the fancy, feminine things we love. Just look at the menu. Have you ever seen so many "girlie" goodies? We created a flowery party atmosphere with big baskets blooming with lilacs, but you could substitute other fresh or dried flowers, or even winter greenery, to reflect the season.

· recipes ·

SPARKLING RASPBERRY LEMONADE
MANGO MINT ICED TEA
ASPARAGUS SALAD *with* CHAMPAGNE VINAIGRETTE
CURRIED CHICKEN TEA SANDWICHES
TOMATO-BASIL TEA SANDWICHES
MINI FRESH FRUIT TARTS

· projects ·

PAPER ROSE SHOWER INVITATIONS
TISSUE PAPER DECORATIONS
GARDEN PARTY HAT CAKE

· getting started ·

· PLANNING TIPS ·

- Don't plan the shower too close to the big event. The bride's schedule is typically very tight in the few weeks leading up to the wedding.

- Ask someone to record each guest's gift as the bride is opening presents.

- Before the shower, ask someone to take snapshots of the festivities, beginning to end. Make sure they get a shot of each guest with the guest of honor. These photos make great thankyou note enclosures.

- The ultimate shower gift? A pretty basket filled with last-minute things a bride may need on her wedding day to ensure it's perfect, like a small sewing kit, aspirin and band-aids, tissues and breath mints.

- Most likely you'll have guests who won't know each other, so make name tags ahead of time for everyone

- Don't forget background music. It helps set the mood and fills any awkward silences when guests are just getting to know each other.

· TO DO LIST ·

- **5-6 Weeks Before:**
  Make and send invitations to out-of-town guests.

- **3-4 Weeks Before:**
  Make and send invitations to local guests.

- **2 Weeks Before:**
  Make sure you have a camera and plenty of film on hand.
  Make shower favors.
  Make tissue paper decorations.

- **1 Week Before:**
  Purchase non-perishables.
  Prepare Champagne Vinaigrette and refrigerate.
  Prepare Pesto Butter and refrigerate.
  Prepare Lemon Curd and refrigerate.

- **Day Before:**
  Buy perishables.
  Prepare Garden Party Hat Cake.
  Prepare Pastry Cream and refrigerate.
  Prepare Curried Mayonnaise and refrigerate.

- **Party Day:**
  Prepare lemonade and iced tea.
  Prepare salad and toss with dressing just before serving.
  Prepare tea sandwiches.
  Assemble tarts.

PAPER ROSE SHOWER INVITATIONS

SUPPLIES

for each invitation:

4-1/4x6-1/4-inch envelope

6x8-inch petal-filled handmade paper

1 sheet mini gingham scrapbooking paper

8-1/2x11-inch sheet ivory or white paper

4x6-inch ivory card stock paper, optional

1 stick-on paper rose

18 inches sheer ribbon

Fine-line marker

Pinking shears

Scissors

Glue stick

Hole punch

Ruler

1. Using pinking shears, cut a 2½-inch square from the gingham paper. Use regular scissors to cut a 2-inch square from the ivory paper. Fold the petal-filled paper into a 4x6-inch rectangle. Glue on the 2½-inch gingham square, then the 2-inch ivory square on top of it. Affix the stick-on paper rose. With the fine-line marker, write the bride's name beneath the rose. Set aside.

2. Using pinking shears, cut a 2x3-inch rectangle from the ivory paper and write your shower information on it with the fine-line marker. With the regular scissors, cut a 4x6-inch rectangle from the gingham paper. Glue the shower information sheet onto the gingham paper and place inside the folded petal-filled paper.

3. Punch two holes close to the fold several inches apart, and thread the ribbon through the holes. Tie a pretty bow and slip the invitation into the envelope. Include the optional ivory card stock if you'll be assembling a Book of Wedding Wisdom.

MAKE A BOOK OF WEDDING WISDOM

To make a shower memento that will last a lifetime, insert a blank 4x6-inch piece of ivory card stock into each invitation. Include a note in each invitation asking guests to write a few words of marriage advice on the blank paper and bring it with them to the shower. At the shower, collect the "words of wisdom" from each guest and slide each page into the plastic sleeves of a plain 4x6-inch photo album. Decorate the album cover to match your invitations, and present it to the lucky bride-to-be.

TISSUE PAPER FLOWER

1. Stack 6 sheets of 8-inch tissue paper and fan fold, as shown.

2. Twist florist wire around the center and fan out the paper on both sides.

3. Starting with the top sheet, pull each sheet toward the center to create an abundance of flower petals.

SUPPLIES

for each 4-inch
Tissue Paper Flower:

6 sheets of 8-inch square
tissue paper
(in your party theme colors)
Florist wire
Scissors

for each 2-inch Rosebud:

10-inch square of white tissue paper
4-inch square of pink tissue paper
3-inch tall pre-cut lavender tissue
paper petal
3-inch tall pre-cut green tissue
paper petal
4-inch pre-cut green tissue
"grass blades"
Florist wire stem
Green florist cloth tape
Waxed florist tape, optional

TISSUE PAPER ROSEBUD

1. Crumple the white tissue paper around the wire stem. Twist to secure.

2. Wrap the pink square of tissue over the white. Twist to secure.

3. Twist on a pre-cut lavender petal, then a pre-cut green petal and grass blade.

4. Wrap with cloth tape, beginning at the place the tissue meets the stem, and working up to the bud. Wrap the remaining stem with waxed florist tape, if desired.

SUPPLIES

2 boxes of your favorite 18.5-ounce cake mix

Two 16-ounce cans of frosting, tinted to
match your party theme colors

1 batch of Royal Icing, recipe on page 50

Pastry tube or zippered plastic bag

2 yards of ribbon for trim

Toothpicks

11x17x2-inch pan

Woven Traditions® Medium
8" Mixing Bowl

Wax paper

Butter and flour

1. Preheat oven to 350°F. Generously grease and flour the medium mixing bowl. Line the 11x17x2-inch pan with wax paper.
2. Prepare both cake mixes according to package instructions.
3. Fill the medium mixing bowl with batter 2½ inches from the top. Bake approximately 35 minutes or until a toothpick inserted into the center comes out clean. Fill the 11x17x2-inch pan with batter to a depth of 1 inch. Bake approximately 22 minutes or until the cake gently springs back when touched in the center. Cool both cakes.
4. To assemble, carefully cut two 11-inch diameter semicircles from the 11x17x2-inch pan. Carefully lift the semicircles out of the pan and position them on a platter to create the brim of the hat. Frost.
5. Invert the mixing bowl, gently shake the cake out and position it in the center of the hat brim. Frost.
6. With the Royal Icing in a pastry tube (or zippered plastic bag with the corner clipped) decorate the hat. We used polka dots but any simple design works well.
7. Use the ribbon to create a hatband and bow; use toothpicks to hold the ribbon in place.

· OUR FAVORITE SHOWER FAVORS ·

1. Tulle wrapped Longaberger® Pint-Size Pillar Candles, as shown.
2. Scented gift soaps, like the pretty woven ones available at Longaberger Homestead.®
3. Small picture frames.
4. Heart shaped cookie cutters.
5. Music CDs.
6. Bundles of notecards decorated with pressed, dried flowers.
7. Chocolate-dipped strawberries in cellophane.
8. Seed packets: Bachelor's Buttons or Baby's Breath.
9. Flower-print gardening gloves and gardeners soap.
10. English lavender sachets.

SPARKLING RASPBERRY LEMONADE

makes 8 servings

Ingredients:

- One 12-ounce can frozen lemonade, defrosted
- ½ cup raspberry flavored syrup, available at coffee shops
- 6 cups sparkling water
- ½ pint fresh raspberries
- Fresh mint sprigs, for garnish

Instructions:

- Place all ingredients except mint in a large pitcher and mix. Pour into tall glasses filled with cracked ice and a few fresh raspberries. Garnish each with a mint sprig.

MANGO MINT ICED TEA

makes 8 servings

Ingredients:

- 4 cups strong mint tea
- 4 cups mango nectar (available in health food stores and larger supermarkets)
- One 12-ounce can frozen lemonade, defrosted
- 4 cups sparkling water
- Fresh mint leaves, for garnish
- 1 mango, skin and pit removed and discarded, sliced into thin strips, for garnish

Instructions:

- Combine the first 4 ingredients in a large pitcher and mix. Serve over cracked ice with a few fresh mint leaves. Thread 1 mango slice onto a skewer or straw and place in each glass.

The most memorable bridal shower activities are those that serve a purpose. Here are a few of our favorites:

DANCE THE DAY AWAY:
Rent an instructional swing-dance video to prepare everyone for the upcoming wedding dance.

CRAFTS TO HELP THE BRIDE:
Help the bride assemble her wedding favors, or fill tulle bags with birdseed to toss at the departing couple at the wedding.

LEARN SOMETHING NEW:
Invite a chef from a favorite restaurant to demonstrate pastry making, then serve the finished pastries. Find an accomplished cake decorator and have her decorate your shower cake right before your guests' eyes. Or call your local community college for names of adult-education instructors who might give your guests a quick course on flower arranging, wine appreciation, yoga or container gardening.

TELL A STORY:
Set a theme for your shower, and ask guests to bring gifts relating to the theme. As each guest's gift is opened, ask her to share a special story about it. For instance, if your shower has a kitchen theme, a guest might bring a gift of a saucepan, along with a recipe for hot fudge sauce and a story or favorite memory relating to the recipe.

ASPARAGUS SALAD WITH CHAMPAGNE VINAIGRETTE

serves 6 to 8

Ingredients:
- 2 pounds fresh asparagus
- One 8 to 9 ounce package frozen peas, defrosted and drained
- 1 English (seedless) cucumber, diced
- 4 scallions, chopped
- 4 hard-boiled egg whites, diced
- 12 radishes, diced
- 2 tablespoons chopped fresh flat-leaf parsley
- 2 tablespoons chopped fresh chives
- ½ cup Champagne Vinaigrette
- Salt and freshly ground black pepper, to taste
- 5 ounces Boursin (savory flavored cheese)

Instructions:
- Snap off and discard the tough, lower portion of each asparagus spear. Slice the asparagus diagonally into 1½-inch pieces.
- Bring a large pot of water to a boil. Drop in the asparagus pieces and cook for 2 minutes. Drain in a colander and rinse with cold water.
- Place the asparagus in a large mixing bowl along with the peas, cucumbers, scallions, egg whites, radishes, parsley and chives; toss gently. Add ½ cup Champagne Vinaigrette and toss again.
- Season with salt and pepper and gently toss again.
- Sprinkle the salad with the Boursin and serve. Salad may be assembled early in the day, but do not toss with the dressing until ready to serve.

CHAMPAGNE VINAIGRETTE

makes 1 cup

Ingredients:
- 2 hard-boiled egg yolks
- 2 tablespoons fresh lemon juice
- 2 tablespoons champagne vinegar
- 2 teaspoons Dijon mustard
- Salt and freshly ground black pepper
- ¾ cup extra-virgin olive oil

Ingredients:
- With a fork or whisk, mash the egg yolks in a medium mixing bowl. Stir in the lemon juice, champagne vinegar, mustard, and salt and pepper, to taste. Add the olive oil in a steady drizzle while whisking continuously. Store refrigerated for up to one week in an airtight container.

• recipes •

CURRIED CHICKEN TEA SANDWICHES

makes 2 dozen sandwiches

Ingredients:
- 24 slices thin white bread
- 1 recipe Curried Mayonnaise
- 1 English (seedless) cucumber, sliced very thin
- 2 whole cooked chicken breasts, bones and skin removed and sliced very thin
- ⅓ cup sliced almonds, toasted and cooled

Instructions:
- Spread the Curried Mayonnaise on two slices of bread. Layer one slice with 4 cucumber disks, 4 or 5 slices of chicken and sprinkle with a few toasted almonds; place the other slice on top.
- Carefully trim the crusts with a serrated knife. Cut in half. Repeat process with the remaining ingredients.
- Place the sandwiches on a tray lined with wax or parchment paper and cover with damp paper towels and then plastic wrap. Store in the refrigerator until ready to serve. The sandwiches may be assembled 2 to 3 hours in advance.

CURRIED MAYONNAISE

makes 1 cup

Ingredients:
- ¾ cup real mayonnaise
- 2 tablespoons curry powder
- ½ teaspoon sea salt
- ¼ cup chutney
- ¼ cup golden raisins (a moister, plumper raisin)

Instructions:
- Combine all ingredients in a small mixing bowl and blend well. Store in an airtight container in the refrigerator. Curried Mayonnaise may be prepared up to 2 days in advance.

makes 16 open-face sandwiches

Ingredients:
- 16 slices thin white sandwich bread
- 2 to 3 tablespoons Pesto Butter
- 3 plum tomatoes, thinly sliced (16 slices total)
- Three 4-ounce balls fresh mozzarella, thinly sliced (16 slices total)
- 16 medium-size fresh basil leaves
- Sea salt
- Olive oil

Instructions:
- Using a round cookie cutter or the rim of a glass, cut a 2-inch circle out of each bread slice.
- Spread one side of cutout with Pesto Butter, top with 1 tomato slice, then 1 mozzarella slice. Finally, add 1 basil leaf and a few crystals of sea salt. Drizzle lightly with the olive oil.
- Tea sandwiches may be assembled 1 hour in advance and placed in the refrigerator. Allow the sandwiches to come to room temperature (about 15 minutes) before serving.

PESTO BUTTER

makes ½ cup

This delicious sandwich spread can also be used to add zesty flavor to sautéed vegetables or grilled chicken breasts.

Ingredients:
- ½ cup (1 stick) unsalted butter, room temperature
- 2 tablespoons pesto spread, available in tubes at Italian groceries, specialty markets or larger supermarkets
- 1 tablespoon chopped fresh parsley

Instructions:
- In a small container, blend the ingredients together using a small spatula or fork. Cover and refrigerate for up to 1 week.

MINI FRESH FRUIT TARTS

makes twenty-four 2½-inch tarts

Ingredients:
- 24 pre-made baked small tart shells
- 1 recipe Lemon Curd Filling or Pastry Cream, recipes on page 91
- 2 to 3 cups fresh berries or assorted seasonal fruits (such as kiwis, strawberries, apricots, bananas, figs) peeled, seeded or sliced
- ½ cup apple jelly
- Confectioners' sugar, optional

Instructions:
- Spoon the desired filling into the tart shells. Arrange fruits on top of the filling. Melt the apple jelly in a microwave-safe bowl 30 to 60 seconds. Brush the fruit with the liquid jelly to add a glossy finish. Lightly dust the tarts with confectioners' sugar, if desired. The tarts may be assembled and refrigerated several hours before serving.

· Elegant Yet Easy ·

Pre-made tart shells, mini phyllo dough shells and lemon curd are all available at larger supermarkets or bakeries. You could also substitute instant vanilla or chocolate pudding for the lemon or cream filling.

Or look to Longaberger Homestead® for our mini tart shells, lemon curd, raspberry lemonade and more. Call our Personal Shopper Line at 1-740-322-5588, option 2, and the friendly folks there will gladly ship your order.

LEMON CURD

makes 2 cups

Ingredients:
- 6 large egg yolks
- 1 cup granulated sugar
- ½ cup fresh lemon juice
- Zest of 1 lemon
- 10 tablespoons unsalted butter, cut into bits

Instructions:
- Place the egg yolks in a heavy nonreactive saucepan. Quickly whisk in the sugar. Add the lemon juice, zest and butter; stir to combine. Cook over medium-low heat, stirring continuously, for 7 to 8 minutes or until the curd comes to a gentle boil.
- Remove from the heat and immediately strain the curd into a nonreactive bowl. Place a sheet of plastic wrap directly onto the curd's surface, and refrigerate for up to 1 week.

PASTRY CREAM

makes 2½ cups

Ingredients:
- 2 cups whole milk
- ½ vanilla bean (pod split in half, seeds scraped free with a knife)
- ½ cup granulated sugar
- 4 large egg yolks
- 2 tablespoons all-purpose flour
- 2 tablespoons cornstarch
- 2 tablespoons unsalted butter
- 2 teaspoons Grand Marnier, optional

Instructions:
- Combine the milk and the split vanilla bean and seeds in a small saucepan. Over medium-high heat, bring the milk to a gentle simmer, then remove from the heat and cover for 10 minutes.
- Place the egg yolks in a heavy nonreactive saucepan and quickly whisk in the sugar. Stir in the flour and cornstarch. Add the milk slowly, whisking continuously until the mixture is smooth.
- Cook over medium heat, stirring continuously until the mixture comes to a gentle boil, about 8 minutes. Allow the mixture to boil for 10 seconds and then remove the pan from the heat. Stir in the butter and the optional Grand Marnier.
- Strain the pastry cream into a nonreactive bowl. Place a sheet of plastic wrap directly onto the Pastry Cream and refrigerate up to 1 day in advance.

· VARIATION ·

Add any of the following to the curd after it has been strained:
· Toasted coconut
· Chopped toasted hazelnuts
· Whipped cream or meringue

SUMMER

You'll be glad to know that, in our part of the country at least, summer hasn't changed. It's still all about sprinklers and sparklers, bare feet and popsicles. Grills get fired up on backyard patios, the neighbors wander over to chat away a warm evening, and kids stay up late to catch fireflies. It's a lovely, lazy time, yet we still have enough energy to organize get-togethers and block parties. Want to know our secrets?

FRIENDS & FOOD
·Al Fresco·

A CASUAL GATHERING OF FRIENDS PAYS TRIBUTE TO THE LAZY DAYS OF SUMMER.

Summer was made for evening entertaining: Mother Nature supplies the ambiance, farmers markets provide the menu, and grills do most of the cooking. Flickering candles and pleasant conversation are all the entertainment required. Easy-going attitudes are mandatory.

· recipes ·

ROASTED RED PEPPER GAZPACHO
with TOASTED CROUTONS
GRILLED HALIBUT *with* CHOPPED OLIVE TAPENADE
GRILLED VEGETABLES *with* CRUMBLED FETA
FRESH BERRY PARFAITS

· projects ·

CHERRY TOMATO PLACE FAVORS
PETALS *and* POTTERY CENTERPIECE
SUMMER POTPOURRI

· getting started ·

· PLANNING TIPS ·

- If summer bugs aren't on your guest list, spray your outdoor entertaining area several hours before party time.

- Be sure to use unscented candles if they'll be lit where food is being served.

- If you're using a gas grill, check the tank a few days beforehand to make sure you have enough fuel.

- Because votive candles only supply so much light after dark, think ahead about how you'll add to the romantic glow. Consider hanging tiny white lights in nearby trees, firing up a few tiki torches or scattering a few vintage lanterns here and there.

· TO DO LIST ·

- **3 Weeks Before:**
  Call guests to invite them to dinner.

- **1-2 Weeks Before:**
  Make follow-up phone calls to guests, if necessary.
  Shop for non-perishables.

- **Day Before:**
  Gather serving pieces and tableware.
  Shop for perishables.
  Assemble Cherry Tomato Place Favors.
  Arrange fresh flowers in Tiny Tote™ Basket.
  Prepare and refrigerate Fresh Berry Parfaits.
  Prepare Chopped Olive Tapenade and refrigerate.
  Prepare Toasted Croutons.

- **Party Day:**
  Clean grill.
  Collect and refrigerate petals for centerpiece.
  Prepare Roasted Red Pepper Gazpacho.
  Prepare vegetables and halibut for grilling.
  Just before guests arrive, arrange Petals and Pottery Centerpiece.
  Kick off shoes.

CHERRY TOMATO PLACE FAVORS

SUPPLIES

Small Dessert Bowls
(one for each guest)

Cherry tomatoes

Produce netting cut
from a bag of potatoes
or oranges

Fresh sprigs of basil

Small ivory sale tags

Natural twine

Pen

1. Write your guests' names on the sale tags with a pen.

2. Bundle a portion of cherry tomatoes (enough to make a nice mound in a Small Dessert Bowl) in a square of the produce netting. Tie the bundle closed with twine.

3. Thread twine onto the name tag and tie with a simple bow.

4. Place the tomato bundles into Small Dessert Bowls, tucking a sprig of fresh basil into each one.

· GOOD IDEA ·

The best cherry tomatoes will, of course, come from your own garden. No garden? For the freshest taste and biggest flavor, search out a roadside produce stand or farmers market for locally grown tomatoes. No time? Look for cherry tomatoes sold on the vine at your favorite grocery store.

ROASTED RED PEPPER GAZPACHO WITH TOASTED CROUTONS

makes 8 cups

Ingredients:
- 6 large red bell peppers
- 3 large vine-ripe tomatoes, peeled and seeded
- 1½ large English (seedless) cucumbers, 1 peeled and cut into 8 pieces; ½ cucumber diced for garnish
- 2 cloves garlic, coarsely chopped
- 2 tablespoons red wine vinegar
- ¼ cup extra-virgin olive oil
- 1½ teaspoons salt
- Freshly cracked black pepper
- 2 tablespoons chopped parsley
- 2 tablespoons snipped chives
- Toasted Croutons

Instructions:
- Place the peppers directly on a hot grill and char all sides. Alternatively, place the peppers on a baking sheet and char under a broiler set on high. Place the charred peppers in a sealed paper bag and allow them to steam for 5 minutes. Using a paring knife, scrape off the blackened skin.
- Slice peppers in half. Remove and discard the seeds and stems. Purée the peppers in a blender or food processor.
- Add the tomatoes, cucumber, garlic, vinegar, and salt and pepper to taste. Blend until smooth. With the processor running, add the olive oil in a steady stream

and mix until incorporated. Season with salt and pepper, to taste. Cover and chill for 2 to 3 hours.
- Whisk the soup briefly before serving. Garnish each portion with the chopped cucumbers, parsley, chives and Toasted Croutons. Serve with Grilled Garlic Toasts.
- This soup is best served the same day it is made.

TOASTED CROUTONS

Ingredients:
- 2 cups cubed fresh sourdough or French bread
- ¼ cup extra-virgin olive oil
- Sea salt and freshly cracked black pepper

Instructions:
- Preheat oven to 350° F. Toss the bread cubes with the olive oil in a medium mixing bowl. Place the bread pieces on a large baking sheet. Sprinkle with salt and pepper, to taste.
- Bake for 12-15 minutes or until the croutons are lightly golden and crunchy. Shake the pan after the first 8 minutes of baking.
- Cool the croutons and store in an airtight container.

GRILLED GARLIC TOASTS

Ingredients:
- Twelve 1-inch slices of sourdough or country French bread
- ⅓ cup extra-virgin olive oil
- 1 head garlic, top inch of the head sliced off
- Sea salt and freshly cracked black pepper

Instructions:
- Prepare a medium-hot grill or turn on the broiler and place the rack in the uppermost part of the oven.
- Brush both sides of each piece of bread with the olive oil and place on a tray. Place the bread on the grill and grill on both sides, until lightly toasted, or broil each side of the bread in the preheated oven to a light golden color.
- Brush one side of each piece of hot toast with the cut side of the garlic. Sprinkle with salt and pepper, to taste.

GRILLED HALIBUT WITH CHOPPED OLIVE TAPENADE

serves 6

Ingredients:

- Six 6- to 8-ounce halibut or Chilean sea bass fillets
- Juice of 1 lemon
- ¼ cup dry white wine
- 4 fresh bay leaves or 1 dry leaf
- 2 shallots, peeled and sliced
- ¼ cup olive oil plus extra for grilling
- Sea salt and freshly cracked black pepper, to taste
- 1 recipe Chopped Olive Tapenade
- Lemon or orange slices and bay leaves for garnish

Instructions:

- Rinse the fillets and remove all pin bones. Pat the fish dry with paper towels and place in a nonreactive dish or pan.
- Prepare the grill, allowing the coals to burn for at least 20 to 30 minutes before cooking the fish. The coals should be covered in a uniform gray, ash color.
- While the grill is heating, combine the lemon juice, white wine, bay leaves, shallots and olive oil in a small mixing bowl. Pour the marinade over the fish and turn once. Refrigerate 15 to 20 minutes.
- Transfer the fish fillets to a baking sheet and drizzle each fillet lightly with oil. Salt and pepper each piece, to taste.
- Before placing the fish on the grill, scrub the metal grate with a wire brush. Using a long pair of tongs, oil the grate with a towel or rag that has been dipped in oil.
- Grill each fillet for 4-6 minutes, then turn the fish over and grill another 4-6 minutes. Remove the fish from the grill. Serve with the Chopped Olive Tapenade and garnish with citrus slices and bay leaves.

CHOPPED OLIVE TAPENADE

makes 1 cup

Ingredients:

- ¾ cup coarsely chopped green olives
- ½ teaspoon yellow mustard seeds
- ¼ teaspoon red pepper flakes
- 2 tablespoons capers
- 2 tablespoons chopped flat-leaf parsley
- Zest of 1 orange
- 2 tablespoons extra-virgin olive oil
- Sea salt and pepper, to taste

Instructions:

- Combine all ingredients in a medium mixing bowl and stir to combine. Tapenade may be prepared several days in advance, covered and stored in the refrigerator.

GRILLED VEGETABLES WITH CRUMBLED FETA

serves 6

Ingredients:

- 2 tablespoons fresh thyme leaves or 2 teaspoons dried thyme
- ½ cup extra-virgin olive oil
- Juice of 2 lemons
- 2 large fennel bulbs
- 3 assorted bell peppers, stem and seeds removed and cut into 2-inch strips
- 1 medium eggplant, sliced into ¾-inch pieces
- 2 medium zucchini, cut into ¾-inch disks
- 2 medium red onions, cut into ½-inch disks
- Sea salt and freshly cracked black pepper, to taste
- ½ cup crumbled feta cheese
- ½ cup toasted pine nuts
- 2 tablespoons chopped flat-leaf parsley
- 2 tablespoons snipped chives

Instructions:

- Whisk together the thyme, olive oil and lemon juice in a small bowl.
- Cut each fennel bulb into 3 or 4 slices. Place in an oven-proof glass container. Add ¼ cup water and cover with a damp paper towel. Microwave for 3 to 5 minutes until the fennel is semi-translucent and slightly pliable.
- Prepare the grill, allowing the coals to burn for at least 30 to 35 minutes. Coals should be medium-hot. Before grilling the vegetables, scrub the metal grate with a wire brush. Then, using a long pair of tongs, oil the grate with a rag that has been lightly dipped in oil.
- Place all of the prepared vegetables on a tray and brush both sides of each piece with the marinade. Sprinkle with salt and pepper, to taste.
- Grill the vegetables about 2 to 3 minutes per side. Transfer to a platter.
- Sprinkle the grilled vegetables with the cheese, nuts and herbs. Season with salt and pepper, to taste.

· Grilling Tips ·

· Clean First, Cook Second

To keep grilled foods from sticking, always prepare the grill grate before each use. Let the grate heat up over the coals for 15-20 minutes, then scrub it with a wire brush.

· Dress To Grill

Never underestimate how hot a grill can get. Protect yourself with grilling gloves and an apron that generously covers your clothing. Long sleeves and closed-toed shoes aren't a bad idea, either.

· Use The Right Tools

Attempt to turn steaks over red-hot coals just once with a dinner fork and you'll see why it's a good idea to invest in a set of long-handled grilling tools.

· Cool It

Keep raw meat, fish and poultry on ice until they're ready to hit the grill.

FRESH BERRY PARFAITS

serves 6

Ingredients:

- 6 cups fresh berries (2 cups each of raspberries, blackberries, blueberries and hulled and sliced strawberries), plus extra for garnishing
- 4 tablespoons granulated sugar
- 2 tablespoons Grand Marnier or other orange liqueur
- ¼ cup fresh lemon juice
- ¼ cup fresh orange juice
- 18 crispy ladyfingers (such as Savoiardi, a crisp Italian sponge biscuit)
- 1 recipe Custard Mousse
- Fresh mint sprigs for garnish

Instructions:

- Gently toss all of the berries (except for those set aside for garnishing) with half of the sugar (2 tablespoons) and all the liqueur. Set aside for 10 minutes.
- To make the syrup, place the remaining 2 tablespoons of sugar, the lemon and orange juices in a shallow, microwave-safe bowl and microwave for 30 to 60 seconds on high, or until the sugar dissolves.
- Place ½ cup of the berries into each of six 12-ounce glasses. Dunk the ladyfingers into the syrup and place 3 biscuits, evenly spaced, around the inside of each glass. (If the biscuits stick up above the rim, gently push them lower into the glass once they have softened.) Add ½ cup of the Custard Mousse to each

glass, gently tapping the glass on the table to settle the mousse and close any gaps. Top with 2 tablespoons of berries and 2 more tablespoons of mousse.
- Cover the glasses with plastic wrap and refrigerate overnight. Before serving, garnish each glass with fresh whole berries and a sprig of mint.

CUSTARD MOUSSE

Ingredients:

- 6 large egg yolks
- ⅓ cup granulated sugar
- 3 tablespoons freshly squeezed orange juice
- ¼ cup Grand Marnier or other orange liqueur
- 1 cup heavy cream
- 1 cup mascarpone cheese
- Zest from 1 orange

Instructions:

- Place the egg yolks in a bowl and quickly whisk in the sugar. Add the juice and liqueur. Place the bowl over a simmering pot of water and cook, stirring constantly, until the mixture is very thick. Do not allow the custard to boil. Remove the bowl from the heat and place it in an ice-water bath; stir to cool it quickly.
- Place the mascarpone in the bowl of an electric mixer and beat for 1 minute. Add the heavy cream and beat until the mixture holds firm peaks. Add the cooled custard and the orange zest and mix just until blended. Cover and refrigerate until you are ready to assemble parfaits.

· W H A T   A ·
Blast!

A SUMMERTIME PARTY THAT BRINGS NEIGHBORS TOGETHER TO CELEBRATE AMERICA.

Block parties come in all shapes and sizes. We prefer those that are large enough to let neighbors get to know neighbors, but not so large that anyone feels lost in the crowd. Start planning six weeks ahead so you'll have plenty of time to get the word out and apply for any permits your city requires. Warning: Do not attempt to host this party yourself. Ask a cross-section of neighbors to help and the process will be as rewarding as the party itself.

· recipes ·

HAMBURGERS *and* HOT DOGS
FIESTA TACO DIP
CRABBY ORZO SALAD
DILLY GARDEN SALAD
GRANDMA BONNIE'S POTATO SALAD
OVERNIGHT VEGETABLE SALAD
AMISH-STYLE BAKED BEANS
PEACH COBBLER
GOLDEN POUND CAKES

· projects ·

LITTLE HOUSE INVITATIONS
PATRIOTIC T-SHIRT DECORATING
BLOCK PARTY MEMORY BOOK

· getting started ·

· PLANNING TIPS ·

- Be prepared for rain. Decide early if your solution will be umbrellas, a covered porch, a garage or an alternate date.

- If you'll be partying in the street, call your city authorities and ask for permission to barricade it. (Kids love the freedom to play in the otherwise-forbidden street.)

- Decide who will bring paper goods, ice, coolers, grills, tables, chairs and trash cans.

- Stock a basket with emergency supplies like adhesive bandages, tissues, moist towelettes, sunscreen and bug spray.

- Block parties are prime trading opportunities. Consider setting aside a table at the party to exchange books, plants, kids clothes or sports equipment. Remember to mention it on your invitation, so guests have plenty of time to gather and organize their trade-ins.

· TO DO LIST ·

- **4-6 Weeks Before:**
  Get together with a group of neighbors to set the date and a rain date.
  Divide responsibilities, including cleanup.
  Apply for permits, barricades, security, etc.

- **3 Weeks Before:**
  Make and deliver invitations.
  Make party reminders.
  Make banner.

- **2 Weeks Before:**
  Shop for paper supplies.

- **1 Week Before:**
  Deliver party reminders.

- **Day Before:**
  Prepare your potluck contribution.
  Collect borrowed coolers and grills from neighbors.

- **Party Day:**
  Set up and decorate party location.
  Pick up ice.
  Bond with neighbors during party.
  Supervise cleanup.

LITTLE HOUSE INVITATIONS

SUPPLIES

for each:

1 yard red, white and blue striped ribbon

One 3x5-inch recipe card

1 sheet 8-1/2x11-inch white cover stock paper

Black marker

Watercolors, crayons or colored markers

Hole punch

Scissors

Photocopier

Delivery crew

1. Draw a simple house with a black marker on white cover stock paper. (The front door should be a little larger than your recipe card.) Write your party information on the front door. Photocopy your house onto white cover stock paper, one house for each invitation needed. Ask your children to help cut them out and decorate.

2. Write, "Please bring the recipe for your potluck dish!" on the recipe card. Align the recipe card with the top of the front door and punch holes through both at the top corners of the front door. Place the recipe card on the back of the invitation. Align the holes on the recipe card with the holes on the front door and insert the ribbon through the holes, creating a swag over the front door. Leave about 16 inches of ribbon above each hole; knot these two ends and then tie a bow. Trim ends as necessary.

3. Recruit your delivery crew to hang an invitation on each door knob in the neighborhood.

• GOOD IDEAS •

RECIPES FOR EVERYONE!

It wouldn't be a potluck if someone didn't exclaim, "This is delicious! Who made it? Can I have the recipe?" Anticipate the inevitable by attaching a blank recipe card to the back of each invitation, along with the request that everyone who brings a dish brings the recipe, too. Delegate someone to collect, compile and distribute the recipes. Add a photo or two from the party to create a memento from an unforgettable summer day

BLOCKS OF INFORMATION

A few days before the big day, it's a good idea to send flyers or e-mails around to remind neighbors of the party's starting time and the things they've volunteered to bring. If you have a bit more time, try this fun idea: Purchase an inexpensive set of children's blocks, jot a short reminder on each, and leave one on each neighbor's door step or front porch.

PATRIOTIC T-SHIRT DECORATING

SUPPLIES

Red, white or blue t-shirts

Cardboard rectangles for stretching (about 2 inches wider than the body of the t-shirt)

Masking tape

Jumbo Idaho potatoes

Star cookie cutters in assorted sizes

Knife

Plastic wrap

Acrylic paints (we used red, white and blue)

Variety of narrow sponge rollers

Variety of flat sponge brushes

Small sponges

Laundry marker or letter stencils

Plastic plates for palettes

Patriotic stamps and stencils, optional

1. In advance, halve the potatoes. Press a star cookie cutter into the flesh of the potato to a depth of ½ inch. With a knife, carve away the potato so that only the star remains. Make lots of these, in different sizes. Cover with plastic wrap and refrigerate.

2. Slip a piece of cardboard into the body of each t-shirt, and tape the sides and/or arms so that the fabric is stretched tightly. Stencil or print with a laundry marker a title on each t-shirt. The t-shirts are now ready for decorating!

3. Set up a t-shirt decorating table so everyone can personalize their own t-shirts. Managing the t-shirt table is a great job for an artistic teenager. Use flat sponge brushes to apply paint to potato stamps. Use small sponges and paint from plastic plates to apply color to stencils. The small rollers are fun for making stripes, and the children will want to use their hands as stamps and stencils. Allow the shirts to dry (about ½ hour) on a clothesline, and then have your own t-shirt parade!

· GOOD IDEA ·

Create a festive summer atmosphere with terra-cotta pots of red geraniums. Stick small flags in the soil to make quick and festive table decorations. Raffle off the pots to help fund next year's block party, and suggest that winners place their flowers in sunny windowsills where the rest of the neighborhood can enjoy them, too!

SUPPLIES

Spiral-bound artist's sketch book
(about 10x14-inches)

Polaroid cameras &
lots of Polaroid film

Waterproof markers in assorted
colors and tip sizes

Caption stickers
(available at camera stores)

Double-sided tape or glue-on photo
corners (available at camera stores)

1. Recruit a resident artist to design your memory book in advance. Rotate the job from year to year.

2. The day of the party, stock a Polaroid photo station with cameras, film, stickers and markers. A sign to suggest three shots per photographer should help with cost control. Encourage guests to add funny captions to their photos either with the stickers or by writing on the bottom panel of each Polaroid with waterproof markers. Collect the photos in a basket and, after the party, affix the photos to the book pages with double-sided tape or photo corners. Leave plenty of room for neighbors to write in their memories.

3. When the Memory Book is completely assembled, share it with your neighbors. Attach a routing list to the inside back cover to make sure everyone gets a chance to see it. Place your name, or the name of next year's Block Party host, at the bottom of the list to ensure its safe return.

· Parties with Spirit ·

What's the secret to a block party everyone will want to repeat next year? Activities! Plan fun things to occupy young kids, more fun things for older kids, and still other activities to be enjoyed by everyone — even grown-ups. Start your party off, for example, with a decorate-your-bike-or-pet parade, or a street hockey match. Dream up your own wacky contests with jump ropes, scooters, Frisbees, jacks, Hula Hoops, bubbles or Twister. Set up checker and chess boards under shady old trees. A Proudly American™ Button Basket filled with sidewalk chalk will allow for artistic expression for the non-competitive. Cool off with squirt guns, lawn sprinklers and water balloons. When darkness falls, bring out the sparklers. See who can catch the most lightning bugs. Don't worry about whether or not people will come to your party. Worry about getting them all to go home!

• All-American Fare •

As long as there have been dads and patios in America, there have been hot dogs and hamburgers on the menu. A byproduct of the American melting pot, hamburgers arrived at Ellis Island in the early 19th century, when immigrants from Germany brought with them their love of "Hamburg-style" steak. The Germans also brought "Dachshund" or "little-dog" sausages, traditionally eaten with bread. After the sausages became popular in 1893 at baseball games and other public events, it didn't take long for Americans to completely adopt "hot dogs" as their very own.

Great stories like these are behind many of America's favorite recipes, and in the pages ahead, you'll find some of our favorite recipes from the *At Home With The Longabergers* recipe book written in 1989 by Rachel Longaberger.

• GOOD TO KNOW •

Get your hot dog and hamburger condiments out of their plastic bottles and jars and into something more attractive, like our Small Dessert Bowls. Tuck the Small Dessert Bowls into their wrought iron Dessert Bowl Caddy to keep them all conveniently located. Finally, transport lettuce, onion and tomato slices to the table all in one trip, piled high in a Bagel Basket with divided protector.

FIESTA TACO DIP

serves 10 to 12

Ingredients:
- One 16-ounce jar black bean dip
- One 16-ounce can black beans, drained and rinsed
- One 4-ounce can chopped chilies, drained
- 2 cups sour cream
- 1 teaspoon chili powder
- ½ teaspoon cumin
- ½ teaspoon paprika
- 1 teaspoon salt
- Two 6-ounce containers prepared guacamole or 2 cups homemade
- One 16-ounce jar salsa or 2 cups homemade
- 2 cups grated white and/or yellow cheddar cheese
- 1 large tomato, seeded and diced
- ½ cup chopped scallions, white and green parts
- One 4-ounce can sliced black olives, drained
- ½ cup diced yellow bell peppers
- Assorted corn chips

Instructions:
- Combine the black bean dip, black beans and chopped chilies in a bowl and mix thoroughly. Spread evenly into the bottom of a 9x13-inch baking dish.
- Combine the sour cream, chili powder, cumin, paprika and salt in a small bowl and mix thoroughly. Place generous spoonfuls of the sour cream mixture, guacamole and salsa over the top of the black bean layer.
- Sprinkle the top of the dip with the cheese, tomatoes, scallions, olives and yellow peppers. Cover and chill in the refrigerator until ready to serve. Serve with big baskets of corn chips.

· GOOD TO KNOW ·

This easy, one-dish appetizer is beautifully presented and good to go when you stash a bag of tortilla chips in the bottom of our Medium Market Basket, and top with our Woven Traditions® 9x13-inch Baking Dish filled with Fiesta Taco Dip. Everyone will fall in love with this wildly clever combination.

CRABBY ORZO SALAD

serves 10

Ingredients:
- ½ pound orzo pasta
- 2 tablespoons olive oil
- 2 cups fresh corn kernels, yellow or white
- 2 cups frozen peas
- ½ cup chopped scallions, white and light green parts only
- ½ cup chopped fresh flat-leaf parsley
- ½ cup chopped fresh cilantro, stems removed
- 1 small bunch fresh chives, cut into 1-inch pieces (½ cup)
- 1 pound fresh backfin lump crabmeat
- Salt and freshly cracked black pepper, to taste
- 1 recipe Lime Dressing

Instructions:
- Bring a large pot of salted water to a boil, add the orzo and cook until al dente, about 5 to 6 minutes. Drain, rinse under cold water and drain again. Place the orzo in a large mixing bowl. Add 2 tablespoons of olive oil and toss to coat.
- In a medium pot, bring 6 cups of salted water to a boil, add the corn and cook for 3 to 5 minutes or until the kernels are tender. Drain the corn in a strainer, saving 3 cups of the hot liquid in a medium mixing bowl. Cool the drained corn on a plate. Add the peas to the hot liquid, let them set for 2 or 3 minutes, then drain and plunge into ice water.
- Toss all the ingredients together in a large mixing bowl. Season with salt and pepper, to taste. The salad may be prepared 1 day in advance but do not toss with the Lime Dressing more than 2 hours before serving.

LIME DRESSING

Ingredients:
- 1 teaspoon red pepper flakes
- ⅓ cup freshly squeezed lime juice
- 2 tablespoons white wine vinegar
- 2 tablespoons honey
- ½ cup extra-virgin olive oil
- ¼ teaspoon ground cumin
- ½ teaspoon salt
- Freshly cracked black pepper, to taste

Instructions:
- Place all the ingredients in a jar with a tight-fitting lid and shake well to combine. Store the jar in the refrigerator for up to 2 days.

• Do Something Patriotic •

One of Rachel Longaberger's fondest memories of growing up in Dresden, Ohio, was attending the annual Memorial Day parade. She says that before the parade started, she'd go to her Grandma Eschman's house to gather flowers. Then she'd walk in the parade, which ended at the town's cemetery. There she'd search among the veterans' graves marked with flags, looking for those with the oldest dates, and decorate those graves with flowers, thinking there was probably no one left living to do so. "It gave me a great appreciation for American history," Rachel recalls. Is there some way you and your neighborhood can commemorate America's veterans, or go beyond the usual flag-waving to show your support for freedom?

DILLY GARDEN SALAD

serves 10

Ingredients:

- 4 cups grated carrots (or two 10-ounce bags grated carrots)
- 1 yellow squash, cut into matchsticks
- 1 fennel bulb (sometimes called anise), stalks discarded and bulb cut into match sticks
- 6 ribs celery, cut into matchsticks
- 4 scallions, white and tender green parts only, thinly sliced
- 1 recipe Dill Dressing
- 6 cups torn mixed salad greens
- Dill sprigs for garnish

Instructions:

- Combine the first 5 ingredients in a large bowl. About 10 minutes before serving, toss with the Dill Dressing.
- Make 3 layers each of the salad greens and the marinated vegetables in a large salad bowl, beginning with the greens and finishing with the vegetables. Garnish with several dill sprigs.

DILL DRESSING

Ingredients:

- 2 tablespoons fresh lemon juice
- 2 tablespoons white balsamic vinegar
- ¼ cup extra-virgin olive oil
- ½ cup plain yogurt
- 2 teaspoons Dijon mustard
- 2 tablespoons sugar
- 2 tablespoons chopped fresh dill
- 1 tablespoon chopped fresh mint
- ¼ teaspoon salt
- Freshly cracked black pepper, to taste

Instructions:

- Place all the ingredients in a jar with a tight-fitting lid. Shake well to emulsify. The dressing may be refrigerated for up to 2 days.

GRANDMA BONNIE'S POTATO SALAD

serves 12 to 14

Ingredients:
- 5 pounds red skin or Yukon gold potatoes
- 4 ribs celery, diced (2 cups)
- 1 large yellow or red onion, diced (1 cup)
- One 4-ounce jar chopped pimentos, drained
- 2 tablespoons snipped fresh chives
- 2 tablespoons chopped fresh flat-leaf parsley
- 5 large hard-boiled eggs, peeled and chopped
- Salt and freshly cracked black pepper, to taste
- 1 recipe Potato Salad Dressing

Instructions:
- Peel and cut the potatoes into bite-size pieces (about 1-inch square). Place the pieces in cold water to keep them from turning brown.
- Over high heat, bring a stockpot of water to boil. Drain the potato pieces and plunge them into the boiling water. Cook until tender, about 7 to 10 minutes. (The time may vary depending on the type and size of potato.) Drain the cooked potatoes and cool completely.
- Place the cooled potatoes, celery, onion, pimento, chives, parsley and chopped eggs in a large mixing bowl; gently toss together.
- Pour 3 cups of the dressing over the potato mixture and gently toss again. Add more dressing, salt or pepper, as desired.
- Cover and chill until ready to serve. Best if made that day.

POTATO SALAD DRESSING

Ingredients:
- 4 large eggs
- 1 cup white vinegar
- 1 cup granulated sugar
- 2 cups mayonnaise

Instructions:
- Whisk together the eggs, vinegar and sugar in a nonreactive saucepan and cook over medium heat, stirring constantly until the sauce thickens, and just reaches a boil. Remove from heat and pour into a bowl. When completely cooled, add the mayonnaise, stirring until well blended.

• A Little Love Story •

Longaberger's founder, Dave Longaberger, learned his appreciation for fine handcrafted baskets from his father, J.W. Famous for his quality and artistry, J.W. made hundreds of baskets for harvesting fruit in the local orchards, and huge baskets for transporting pieces of pottery. In the hours after his regular job at the local paper mill, J.W. also crafted baskets for his family. In the days before plastic bags and cardboard boxes, he made his wife, Bonnie, all kinds of beautiful baskets for countless uses around the house, including baskets for laundry, for berry-picking, for vegetable-gathering, even baskets for storing garden bulbs. Bonnie says her favorite of all J.W.'s handcrafted designs was her Cake Basket. She carried her cakes to church suppers in it, and her friends admired it so much they had to have J.W. make Cake Baskets for them, too. Today, Longaberger's Cake Basket remains a favorite of potluck-goers. In addition to toting layer cakes, this two-handled helper also accommodates our Woven Traditions® Large Mixing Bowl filled with your favorite Potato Salad.

OVERNIGHT VEGETABLE SALAD

serves 10

Ingredients:

- 1 head cauliflower, broken into small florets (4 cups), core discarded
- 1 head broccoli, florets broken into small pieces (about 4 cups)
- 1 green bell pepper, diced (1 cup)
- 1 red onion, minced (1 cup)
- 1 cup mayonnaise
- 2 tablespoons granulated sugar
- ⅓ cup white vinegar
- 1½ teaspoons Dijon mustard
- Salt and freshly cracked black pepper, to taste

Instructions:

- Place the prepared vegetables in a large mixing bowl.
- Whisk together the mayonnaise, sugar, vinegar and mustard in a small mixing bowl. Pour over the vegetables and gently toss.
- Seal the vegetables in an airtight container or plastic bag, and refrigerate overnight. Season with salt and pepper, to taste. Keep chilled until ready to serve.

AMISH-STYLE BAKED BEANS

serves 10

Ingredients:

- 4 slices uncooked bacon, diced
- 2 small onions, diced (1 cup)
- One 16-ounce can red kidney beans, drained
- One 16-ounce can butter beans, drained
- One 16-ounce can navy beans, drained
- 1 cup light brown sugar
- 1 cup ketchup
- 1 teaspoon dry mustard

Instructions:

- Preheat oven to 350°F. Lightly mist a 1½-quart casserole dish with vegetable oil spray.
- Cook the bacon in a medium-size skillet over medium-high heat for 3 to 5 minutes just until the bacon has rendered its fat; do not allow it to brown. Add the onion and cook for 2 to 3 more minutes until it becomes translucent.
- Place the bacon, onions and all three kinds of beans in a large mixing bowl. In a small bowl, stir together the brown sugar, ketchup and mustard. Stir into the bean mixture.
- Pour the beans into the prepared casserole dish and bake, uncovered, for 1 hour.
- Beans may be prepared up to 2 days in advance and reheated before serving.

PEACH COBBLER

serves 8

Ingredients:

- 6 cups sliced fresh peaches (or frozen peaches, defrosted)
- ½ cup granulated sugar
- 2 tablespoons instant tapioca
- 1 cup all-purpose flour
- 1 teaspoon baking powder
- Pinch of salt
- 1 large egg
- ½ cup unsalted butter, melted

Instructions:

- Preheat oven to 350°F. Lightly mist the bottom of a 9-inch pie plate with vegetable oil spray.
- Combine the peaches, sugar and tapioca in a large mixing bowl. Let set for 15 minutes, stirring twice.
- In a medium mixing bowl, combine the flour, baking powder and salt. Add the egg and the melted butter; mix until the batter just begins to come together.
- Pour the peach mixture into the prepared pie plate. Drop small clumps of the batter over the top of the peaches (the batter will not cover them completely).
- Bake 40 to 50 minutes, or until the bubbling juices are thick and the crust is a light golden brown. Check the cobbler after 35 minutes of baking; if the crust is browning too quickly, loosely cover the cobbler with aluminum foil.
- Cool 30 minutes before serving. This dessert is best served the day it is made.

· GOOD IDEA ·

Out of time and in need of a potluck contribution? You can't go wrong with simple summertime favorites like corn on the cob (just throw it on the grill), chewy fresh breadsticks or slices of ice-cold watermelon.

GOLDEN POUND CAKES

makes 2 loaves

Ingredients:
- 2 cups flour
- One pound confectioners' sugar
- Pinch of salt
- 1½ cups (3 sticks) unsalted butter, softened
- 6 eggs, room temperature
- 1 teaspoon almond extract
- 1 teaspoon vanilla extract
- Assorted fresh berries
- Whipped cream, optional

Instructions:
- Preheat oven to 350°F. Grease and flour two 5x9-inch loaf pans.
- Mix the flour, confectioners' sugar and salt in a mixing bowl.
- Cut in the butter until the mixture is crumbly and resembles coarse cornmeal.
- In a small bowl, mix together the eggs and almond and vanilla extracts. Add to the flour mixture and beat for 2 minutes on medium speed.
- Pour batter into prepared loaf pans. Bake at 350°F for 50 to 55 minutes, or until a toothpick inserted into the center of each loaf comes out clean. Cover with foil during the last 10 minutes to prevent over-browning.
- Cool in the pans for a few minutes. Invert onto wire rack to cool completely.
- Top with berries and optional whipped cream.

> **· GOOD TO KNOW ·**
>
> An assortment of berries and whipped cream makes a simple, elegant contribution to any potluck. We like to transport and serve ours in four Woven Traditions® Salt™ Crocks set into a Longaberger Cake Basket with wood riser. The basket holds the crocks more securely than a tray, and stands head and shoulders above the other sweets presented on plates and platters.

FALL

Fall is fun! There are piles of leaves to jump in, pumpkins to carve and shiny new school shoes to buy. But with days getting shorter, there's no time to waste if you're going to plan the best tailgate party of the season, conjure up a Halloween party for all the little ghosts and goblins, or discover new traditions to add to your Thanksgiving feast. Pull on a sweater, grab a cup of cocoa and read on!

HALLOWEEN
Fun!

A KIDS' CELEBRATION THAT MAKES FACES
LIGHT UP LIKE JACK-O-LANTERNS.

Bales of hay, shocks of corn and a jumble of market-stand pumpkins are all you need to set the mood for this fresh-air Halloween celebration. Costumed children are running giddily about, and picnic tables are laden with enticing snacks and fun things for little hands to do. And in the middle of it all, there's you, having as great a time as the kids. Imagine that.

· recipes ·

MAKE-A-FACE PIZZAS
PUMPKIN FACE CUPCAKES
NUTTY CARAMEL APPLES
CRUNCHY MUNCHIES
GHOST TOASTIES

· projects ·

SPOOKY SPIDER INVITATIONS
SPOOKY SPIDER PLACE CARDS
SLUGS & BUGS GOODY BAGS
TERRIBLY CRAFTY PUMPKIN HEADS

· getting started ·

· PLANNING TIPS ·

- Be sure to enlist the help of a few other grown-ups to divide and conquer party prep jobs and guest round-up. If there aren't enough adults to go around, consider paying a few good-natured teens to help out.

- Plan a simple activity for kids to do while they're waiting for other guests to arrive. It may be as simple as spreading craft paper across picnic tables, and asking kids to color the "tablecloth."

- Because children aren't exactly proficient at waiting their turn, have more than one party activity going at a time. Use an ink stamp pad and the Halloween stamp of your choice and let the children dress up plain paper napkins. Kids this age love stamps on their hands and faces too, so bestow them generously on all party participants.

· TO DO LIST ·

- **3 Weeks Before:**
  Make and send Spooky Spider Invitations.

- **1-2 Weeks Before:**
  Shop for groceries and supplies.
  Assemble Slugs & Bugs Goody Bags.
  Mix and store Crunchy Munchies and
  Ghost Toasties.
  Bake and freeze cupcakes for decorating.
  Make Spooky Spider Place Cards.

- **Day Before:**
  Prepare Nutty Caramel Apples.
  Defrost Cupcakes.

- **Party Day:**
  Prepare Make-A-Face Pizzas.
  Set up and decorate party location.
  Have fun!

SPOOKY SPIDER INVITATIONS

SUPPLIES

Orange
construction paper

Black
construction paper

Square envelopes

Paper glue

Gel pens

Scissors

Hobby knife for
an adult

1. Cut a rectangle of orange paper to fit loosely inside your envelope when folded in half. With the help of an adult, cut out a simple Jack-O-Lantern face for the cover using the hobby knife.

2. On scrap paper, design a spider body that fits inside your square. Trace your template onto black construction paper and cut it out.

3. For each spider, make five long strips of paper—four for the legs plus one accordion strip. Glue on all the legs. Then glue one end of the accordion strip to the back of the spider and the other to the inside of the orange card.

4. Write party information on the spider's body with a gel pen. Fold in the legs, fold the card, and place in an envelope.

please come to my
Halloween Party
Alex's House · Oct 31 · 4:30pm

SUPPLIES

Five fuzzy black
pipe cleaners for
each place card

Orange
construction paper

Black marker

Scissors

1. Crisscross three of the pipe cleaners for legs.

2. Coil one pipe cleaner to make the body of the spider.

3. With the remaining pipe cleaner attach the body to the legs. Just wrap and twist between the head and body. This pipe cleaner will become the front set of legs, holding the place card.

4. Bend the back legs so that your spider will stand. Adjust the front legs to hold the place card.

SLUGS & BUGS GOODY BAGS

makes 12 goody bags

Ingredients:
- 2 cups (12 ounces) gummy worms
- 2 cups (12 ounces) chocolate covered banana chips
- 2 cups (12 ounces) Tootsie Roll midgets, unwrapped
- 2 cups (10 ounces) chocolate covered crispies or chocolate covered raisins
- 2 cups French burnt peanuts, Boston Baked Beans, or red jellybeans
- 1 cup (4 ounces) shelled peanuts
- 1 cup (4 ounces) raisins

SUPPLIES

Twelve 9-inch cellophane bags or twelve 12-inch squares of clear or orange cellophane

12 pipe cleaner strips (as shown) or 12 pieces of yarn, 7 to 8 inches in length

12 nametags, optional

Instructions:
- Toss all the treats together. Scoop 1 cup into each bag or into the middle of each cellophane square. Twist the bag or gather the cellophane around the mixture and tie with the pipe cleaner or yarn. Tie a nametag or Halloween message onto each bag.

• Halloween at Longaberger Homestead® •

The Longaberger Company is based in a rural area of central Ohio, where harvest celebrations are time-honored traditions. Each year in October, we decorate The Crawford Barn™ at Longaberger Homestead and invite our employees and neighbors to bring their families over for our much-anticipated Boo Breakfast. Princesses, superheroes and goblins alike take part in interactive stories with costumed characters. There are pumpkins to decorate, photos to pose for, and of course, a Halloween souvenir to take home. Call our Guest Relations Specialist Line at 1-740-322-5588, option 0 to learn more.

PUMPKIN FACE CUPCAKES

makes 12 Small Dessert Bowl cupcakes or 24 traditional cupcakes

Ingredients:

- Brownie or cake mix, or your favorite recipe
- White frosting, canned or your favorite recipe
- Food coloring, optional
- Black licorice sticks cut into 1-inch pieces
- Candy corn
- M&Ms
- Black licorice whips
- Colored sprinkles
- Fruit leather cut into triangles, circles or squares

Instructions:

- Prepare brownie or cake mix according to the package directions, and bake in Woven Traditions® Small Dessert Bowls or in muffin tins filled with paper cupcake liners. Cool completely before decorating.
- If you'd like a range of colors, mix drops of food coloring into the basic white frosting. Frost each cupcake using a small knife. To create the pumpkin stem, insert a 1-inch piece of the licorice stick in the top center of each cake.
- Place the other assorted candies into a divided protector and let guests create their own pumpkin faces.

NUTTY CARAMEL APPLES

makes 12 *apples*

Ingredients:

- 12 flat wooden craft sticks
- 12 large paper cupcake liners
- 1 tray lined with wax paper, misted with vegetable spray
- 2 pounds vanilla caramels, unwrapped
- 5 tablespoons milk or water
- 12 medium apples, your favorite variety
- 2 cups finely chopped peanuts or other favorite nut
- 2 cups colored sprinkles

Instructions:

- Insert 2 inches of a wooden stick into the stem end of each apple.
- Melt together the caramels and milk, stirring until smooth and creamy either in the microwave oven on lowest power or in a double boiler over medium heat.
- Dunk each apple into the warm caramel. As you lift the apple out of the caramel, turn it, allowing some caramel to drip back into the pot.
- Immediately roll the caramel apple in the chopped nuts or sprinkles, and then place it on the prepared tray. Once the caramel has hardened slightly, set each finished apple inside a cupcake liner.

CRUNCHY MUNCHIES

makes 8 to 10 cups

Ingredients:
- Pretzel sticks
- Goldfish pretzels
- Shelled peanuts, plain or honey-roasted
- Mini bagel chips, plain or flavored
- Potato sticks
- Small cheddar crackers
- Sesame sticks
- Rice crackers
- Cheese curls
- Small corn chips

Instructions:
- Choose 4 or 5 snacks from the list above. Measure 2 cups of each ingredient and gently toss them together in a large bowl.

· GOOD IDEA ·

These sweet and salty snacks are perfect take along treats for your on-the-go lifestyle. Pack them in zippered plastic bags for an after-game or school-time snack. Pour into baskets with protectors and serve stylishly.

GHOST TOASTIES

makes 8 cups

Ingredients:
- ½ cup butterscotch chips
- ⅓ cup creamy peanut butter
- 2 tablespoons unsalted butter
- 5 cups cinnamon toast cereal squares
- 1½ cups confectioners' sugar
- 1 cup (6 ounces) yogurt-covered raisins or peanuts
- 1 cup (6 ounces) white chocolate chips
- 1 cup (2 ounces) miniature marshmallows

Instructions:
- In a microwave-safe bowl melt the chips, peanut butter and butter in a microwave on low power for 1 to 2 minutes. Mix until smooth. Do not overcook. (The mixture also can be prepared in a double boiler.)
- In a large bowl, pour the butterscotch mixture over the cereal, and toss to coat evenly.
- Place the confectioners' sugar in a large paper or plastic bag and add the coated cereal squares. Toss until all of the squares are white. Spread the squares on a tray lined with wax paper and allow to dry for 1 hour.
- Combine the coated cereal and the 3 remaining ingredients in a large serving bowl. The mixture will stay fresh in an airtight container for 2-3 days.

·ALWAYS GOOD·
to Go

A TAILGATE PARTY THAT BRINGS FRIENDS TOGETHER.

The real beauty of a tailgate party (besides the perfect Indian Summer weather) is that, because everything must be prepared in advance, you have no choice but to relax and enjoy your own party. It's the best excuse we know of for getting together with old friends. And it's the ideal test of Longaberger's ability to organize, pack, transport and serve wherever you decide to entertain. After all, a tailgate opens in a park, alongside a country road, or overlooking a sunny shoreline as easily as it opens in a crowded parking lot on game day.

· recipes ·

GARDEN CRUNCH SANDWICHES

ALSATIAN CHICKEN SANDWICHES *with*
CARAMELIZED ONION-APPLE MAYONNAISE

VEGETABLE TRAYS *with* CAESAR DIP

CHILLED PENNE SALAD

FRESH FRUIT SKEWERS

CHOCOLATE PECAN BARS

· projects ·

MAGNETIC PHOTO COLLAGE

· recipes ·

GARDEN CRUNCH SANDWICHES

makes 4 sandwiches

Ingredients:

- 4 oblong seeded rolls (approximately 3x5-inches)
- 1 recipe House Vinaigrette or ¼ cup favorite bottled vinaigrette
- 1 cup prepared hummus
- ¼ cup minced scallions
- 2 cups torn mixed salad greens
- ½ cup slivered Kalamata olives
- ½ medium cucumber, diced (1 cup)
- 1 cup roasted red peppers, diced (12-ounce jar)
- 1 cup loosely packed flat leaf parsley, coarsely chopped
- 2 tablespoons chopped fresh basil
- 2 ounces feta cheese, crumbled
- 2 Roma tomatoes, halved, then sliced into 6 pieces each

Instructions:

- Cut each roll horizontally, slicing all but the last ½ inch so that the top and bottom pieces will be hinged. Scoop out some of the soft bread from both the top and bottom, leaving the crust intact. Brush the inside of each sandwich (top and bottom) with the House Vinaigrette.
- Combine the hummus and the scallions in a mixing bowl and spread 4 tablespoons inside each sandwich.
- Toss the lettuce, olives, cucumbers, red peppers, parsley and basil with the remaining vinaigrette and distribute the salad mixture among the rolls.
- Tuck the tomato slices along the outer edge and sprinkle each sandwich with feta cheese.
- Roll each sandwich in wax or parchment paper and keep cool. To make certain the contents stay crunchy, sandwiches should be assembled no more than 2 hours in advance.

HOUSE VINAIGRETTE

Ingredients:

- 2 tablespoons red wine vinegar
- 4 tablespoons olive oil
- ½ teaspoon minced garlic
- 1 teaspoon Dijon mustard
- ¼ teaspoon salt
- ¼ teaspoon freshly cracked black pepper

Instructions:

- Whisk together all ingredients. House Vinaigrette may be made several days in advance and refrigerated in a sealed jar.

· GOOD IDEA ·

There's nothing like a rollicking tailgate party for building pre-game excitement. On the other hand, a post-game party is more relaxed. It's quieter without the crowds, you avoid the mass exodus, and it gives you and your guests a chance to relive the game. So why not do both? Just save the desserts and coffee for after the game. (And be sure to remind guests to come back!)

ALSATIAN CHICKEN SANDWICHES WITH CARMELIZED ONION-APPLE MAYONNAISE

makes 4 sandwiches

Ingredients:

· 1 loaf sourdough bread (3x18-inches) or 4 sourdough rolls (3x5-inches)
· 1 recipe Caramelized Onion-Apple Mayonnaise
· 4 grilled or roasted chicken breasts (about 1 pound), thinly sliced
· 8 slices bacon, cooked and drained (apple-wood smoked or regular bacon)
· 2 ounces white cheddar or Emmentaler cheese, sliced with a vegetable peeler
· 1 cup thinly chopped green cabbage or green leaf lettuce

Instructions:

· If using a loaf rather than the rolls, cut it into 4 equal pieces. Cut each piece horizontally, slicing all but the last ½ inch so that the top and bottom pieces are hinged. Scoop out some of the soft bread from both the top and bottom, leaving the crust intact.
· Toss the sliced chicken with the Caramelized Onion-Apple Mayonnaise. Taste and season with salt and pepper, if necessary. Fill each roll with an equal portion of the chicken mixture and 2 slices of the bacon.
· Top each sandwich with several peels of cheese and a sprinkling of cabbage or lettuce.

· Roll each sandwich individually in wax or parchment paper. Sandwiches, kept cool, may be assembled several hours in advance.

CARAMELIZED ONION-APPLE MAYONNAISE

Ingredients:

· 1 tablespoon unsalted butter
· 1 large yellow onion, diced
· 1 Granny Smith apple, peeled, cored and diced
· 1 tablespoon cider vinegar
· 1 cup mayonnaise
· 3 tablespoons whole-grain mustard
· ½ teaspoon salt
· 1 teaspoon freshly cracked black pepper

Instructions:

· Melt the butter in a medium sauté pan over medium heat until the butter foams. Add the onions and cook for 5 minutes or until translucent. Add the apple bits and cook for 5 to 7 minutes or until the apples and onions caramelize. Add the cider vinegar and cook for another 30 seconds. Remove from the heat and cool completely.
· Combine the remaining ingredients with the cooled apple-onion mixture. This mayonnaise may be prepared 1 day in advance and stored, covered, in the refrigerator.

VEGETABLE TRAYS WITH CAESAR DIP

Hints:

· A variety of easy-to-maneuver shapes add visual interest to vegetable trays.

· For best results, vegetable trays can be prepared several hours in advance and covered with damp paper towels and plastic wrap. Or, to prepare one day in advance, wrap the prepared vegetables in damp paper towels and place in plastic bags, then into the refrigerator.

Two favorite combinations:

GREEN AND WHITE VEGETABLES:

· Cauliflower florets
· Zucchini sticks
· Jicama sticks
· Belgian endive spears
· Anise (also known as fennel) strips

· Broccoli florets
· Asparagus spears } *see Good Idea!*
· Green beans

ANTIPASTO PLATE:

· Zucchini sticks
· Trimmed scallions
· Red or yellow teardrop tomatoes
· Green or black olives
· Marinated artichoke hearts
· Peels of Parmesan cheese or rolled sliced provolone cheese

· Bell pepper slices
· Stuffed hot peppers

CAESAR DIP

makes 1¼ cups

Ingredients:

· ½ cup mayonnaise
· ½ cup sour cream
· ¼ cup chopped scallions
· 1 teaspoon minced garlic
· 2 tablespoons freshly squeezed lemon juice
· ½ cup freshly grated Parmesan cheese
· ½ teaspoon freshly cracked black pepper
· 2 tablespoons fresh chopped parsley

Instructions:

· Combine all ingredients in a mixing bowl. Add salt and pepper, to taste.

> · **GOOD IDEA** ·
>
> Blanch broccoli florets, asparagus spears and green beans to slightly soften and to set their bright green color. Blanch by plunging them into boiling water for 30 to 60 seconds. Drain and plunge into a bowl of ice-cold water. Allow the vegetables to cool before draining thoroughly.

· GOOD IDEA ·

If you're planning a tailgate homecoming reunion, rekindle memories with popular music from pre-graduation days. If your crowd is large and it's not practical to provide camp chairs for everyone, collect vintage wool blankets from yard sales and thrift stores. Bundle them into a big basket like our Large Storage Solutions™ or Large Boardwalk™ Basket, and keep them handy for guests to spread on the ground and on stadium bleachers.

CHILLED PENNE SALAD

serves 12

Pasta Ingredients:
· 1 pound penne, ziti or fusili cooked, drained
· ¼ cup olive oil
· ⅓ cup chopped scallions
· ½ cup chopped fresh basil
· ½ cup chopped fresh flat-leaf parsley
· ½ cup freshly grated Parmesan cheese
· ½ cup pine nuts, toasted
· ½ cup Kalamata olives, pitted and slivered
· 1 cup diced red bell pepper
· 1 cup diced zucchini

Dressing Ingredients:
· 2 tablespoons fresh lemon juice
· 2 tablespoons red wine vinegar
· 1 teaspoon chopped garlic
· ½ teaspoon red pepper flakes
· ½ teaspoon salt
· 1 teaspoon freshly cracked black pepper
· ½ cup extra-virgin olive oil

Instructions:
· Combine all of the pasta ingredients in a large mixing bowl.
· In another bowl, whisk together all the dressing's ingredients except the olive oil.
· Drizzle the oil into the dressing mixture, whisking steadily until well blended and an emulsion forms.
· Pour the dressing over the pasta ingredients, toss lightly.
· Add salt and pepper, to taste.

FRESH FRUIT SKEWERS

Ingredients:

- Strawberries, stems removed
- Seedless grapes, any color
- Fresh figs cut into halves
- Plums, each pitted and cut into 8 pieces
- Kiwis, each peeled and cut into 6 pieces
- Pineapple, trimmed, cored, cut into 1½-inch pieces
- Cantaloupe and honeydew melon, peeled, seeded and cut into 1½-inch chunks
- Juice of 1 lime, per 20 skewers
- 1 tablespoon chopped fresh mint leaves, per 20 skewers
- 6-inch wooden skewers

Instructions:

- Choose 3 or 4 fruits listed. Thread pieces of each fruit to fill 6-inch wooden skewers. These can be assembled 2 to 3 hours before serving, covered with damp paper towels, and placed in the refrigerator.
- Arrange the skewers on a serving tray. Squeeze lime juice over each skewer and sprinkle with the chopped mint leaves.
- Note: The fruit pieces may be prepared the night before. Place the pieces on a tray lined with plastic wrap in a single layer and drape with damp paper towels. Cover well with plastic wrap and refrigerate.

> **· GOOD IDEA ·**
>
> Party guests love fruit skewers because they are fresh and colorful; you'll love them because you can make a variation of this recipe and freeze them the night before. Fruits such as pineapple, mango, bananas and papaya can be cut into pieces, skewered and frozen. Defrost the fruit skewers for about 10-12 minutes before serving. Arrange the fruit skewers on a protector-lined Small Serving Tray Basket, and they will be perfectly thawed just in time for your guests' arrival!

CHOCOLATE PECAN BARS

makes 24 bars

Filling Ingredients:
- 3 cups pecans
- 2 large eggs
- ¾ cup light brown sugar
- ¾ cup light corn syrup
- 1 teaspoon pure vanilla extract
- ¼ cup unsalted butter, melted
- 2 tablespoons all-purpose flour
- 3 ounces semi-sweet chocolate, melted

Chocolate Drizzle Ingredients:
- 2 ounces semi-sweet chocolate
- 2 tablespoons unsalted butter

Instructions:
- Prepare 1 recipe of the Bar Cookie Crust. Preheat oven to 350°F.
- For the filling, toast the pecans at 350°F for 7 minutes or until they give off a nutty aroma. Cool completely and then finely chop.
- Combine the eggs, brown sugar, corn syrup and vanilla in a medium mixing bowl and whisk until smooth. Stir in the butter and flour. Fold in the melted chocolate and the pecans. Pour this over 1 recipe of the baked Bar Cookie Crust, gently spreading to cover the top evenly.
- Return the pan to the oven and bake for 30 to 35 minutes at 350°F or until the topping is firm. Cool completely.
- For the drizzle, combine the chocolate and butter in an ovenproof bowl and microwave on the lowest power for 40 seconds. Stir, and microwave for an additional 20 seconds. Stir again until smooth. Drizzle the chocolate glaze over the bar cookies. Refrigerate for at least 30 minutes before cutting into squares.

BAR COOKIE CRUST

makes one 9x13-inch crust

Ingredients:
- 1 cup (2 sticks) unsalted butter, chilled
- ½ cup confectioners' sugar
- 2 cups all-purpose flour

Instructions:
- Preheat oven to 350°F. Mist a 9x13-inch pan with vegetable oil spray.
- For the crust, beat the butter and sugar in the bowl of an electric mixer or with a hand mixer until smooth and creamy. Add the flour and mix until just incorporated; the dough should just begin to form a ball.
- Press the dough in an even layer over the bottom of the prepared pan. Poke holes in the dough with a fork. Bake for 15 minutes, and remove from oven.

· getting started ·

· TO DO LIST ·

- **3 Weeks Before:**
  Take head count, make Autumn Branch Place Cards.

- **1-2 Weeks Before:**
  Clean the crystal.
  Shop for non-perishable ingredients.
  Order the turkey.
  Make pie dough and freeze.

- **3-4 Days Before:**
  Begin to defrost the turkey if using a frozen bird.

- **2 Days Before:**
  Iron linens and count flatware and dishes.
  Purchase perishable ingredients.
  Defrost pie dough and roll out to fit into pie plates, cover and refrigerate.
  Make Zesty Orange Cranberry Sauce.

- **Day Before:**
  Set the table.
  Choose serving dishes and utensils necessary for the meal.
  Arrange flowers, foliage and fall berries in Small Gatehouse® Baskets.
  Blanch and refrigerate green beans in preparation.
  Prepare Chestnut Dressing.
  Prepare turkey for roasting and return it to the refrigerator.
  Prepare Baked Maple Sweet Potatoes.
  Assemble and bake Apple Blackberry Crumble Pie.
  Assemble and bake Rachel's Favorite Pumpkin Pie.

- **Thanksgiving Day:**
  Roast the turkey, and allow it to set for at least 20 minutes before carving. This will give you some time to organize the side dishes as they finish cooking. Finish the side dishes as needed.

AUTUMN BRANCH PLACE CARDS

SUPPLIES

3-inch square
of paper

1/2-inch wide
organza ribbon

Branches with
leaves and berries
(real or silk)

Calligraphy marker

Scissors

Hole punch

1. Fold squares of paper in half. To give place cards a torn edge, hold the paper down with a ruler and rip ⅛ inch off of each edge.

2. With the hole punch, punch a hole through the folded card. Write guests' names on cards with the calligraphy marker.

3. Insert organza ribbon and tie a pretty bow in the front.

4. Arch the branch under the tented card and arrange the berries for visual balance.

" PLACES EVERYONE"

Place cards can feel stuffy at other times of the year, but at Thanksgiving, they just seem to add elegance to the occasion. If you like the idea of adding seasonal color to your table with Small Gatehouse® Baskets hung over chair backs, as we've done, you could personalize each basket with a name tag. Another option is to simply write names on autumn leaves with a gold paint pen. And here's an idea we love that assigns both place and thanks: Have each guest draw another guest's name from a basket. Then give each guest a small piece of paper, with instructions to write a short reason why they're thankful for the person whose name they drew. Each note goes into a small envelope that becomes the "grateful-for" guest's place card. Open and read (aloud or not) at the table just before the turkey makes its appearance.

· WHAT'S IN YOUR · GATEHOUSE?

These roly-poly-bottomed baskets were inspired by gatehouses; homes usually so small that many of life's necessities must be hung on walls. Because of their simple yet unconventional shape, our Gatehouse® Baskets make uncommonly beautiful centerpieces (think cornucopias), and they're equally spectacular hung on a door or banister holding whatever the season brings. Daffodils in spring? Zinnias in summer? Dried grasses in autumn and holly in winter? It all depends on what's available in your neighborhood and what strikes your fancy. Here we've decked out Small Gatehouse Baskets with oak leaves, twigs, and a few whimsical touches from the craft store, but you may find your favorite fillings right in your own backyard. Better yet, why not pile everyone into the car one spectacular fall day, and spend the afternoon tramping through the woods and checking out roadside stands for fine fillers for your Small Gatehouse Baskets?

BOUNTIFUL CHAIR BASKETS

SUPPLIES

Small Gatehouse Baskets

Protectors

Florist "oasis" foam for each basket

Autumn leaves on branches (we used oak)

Autumn berry branches: bittersweet, rose hips, berry clusters or grapes

Dried eucalyptus

1. Cut florist foam to fit inside basket's protector. Insert foam into the protector, then into the basket. Arrange branches as "high points" and berries as "low points."

2. Fill the center of the arrangement with autumn leaves. Add a few sprigs of eucalyptus for color contrast.

3. Create a focal point with berry clusters or grapes front and center.

ROASTED TURKEY WITH GRAVY

serves 10

Turkey Ingredients:

· One 16- to 18-pound fresh or frozen turkey (if using a frozen bird, remember it may take up to 2 to 3 days in the refrigerator to completely thaw. Thaw the bird in its wrappings).
· Salt and freshly ground black pepper
· 2 medium apples, quartered
· 2 small onions, quartered
· 10 sprigs fresh thyme
· 6 fresh sage leaves
· 2 tablespoons olive oil
· 1 cup chicken or turkey stock
· 1 recipe Browned Sage Butter, page 146
· Cotton kitchen twine

Instructions:

· Remove the giblets and neck. Save the neck for making the gravy. Rinse turkey outside and inside until the water runs clear. Pat dry both inside and outside of the bird. Snip off the wing tips, and season the inside of the turkey with a generous amount of salt and pepper. Stuff the cavity of the bird with the apples, onions, thyme and sage leaves. Tie the legs together with kitchen twine forcing the wings to be pressed against the breast. Allow the bird to sit out of the refrigerator 30 minutes prior to roasting.

· Preheat oven to 400°F. Place a roasting rack in a shallow pan and spray or brush all surfaces with vegetable oil. Position the turkey, breast side up, in the rack. Brush the entire turkey with the olive oil and sprinkle generously with the salt and black pepper.
· Place the turkey in the lower middle area of the oven, uncovered, and cook for 15 minutes. Turn the pan around and cook for 15 minutes more. Lower the oven to 325°F and roast for about 3 to 3½ additional hours. (See Turkey Tips on page 146.) Baste with chicken stock and pan drippings every 30 minutes and then with the Browned Sage Butter the last hour of cooking. If the turkey is browning too quickly cover it loosely with aluminum foil.
· The turkey is done when a thermometer inserted into the thickest part of the thigh reads 180°F. Test for doneness by piercing the thigh with the point of a sharp knife. The juices should run clear.
· Remove the turkey from the oven and allow to set for 20 minutes. Transfer the bird to a cutting board, remove the kitchen twine and carve. Arrange on a platter and garnish.

Turkey Gravy Ingredients:

· 1 tablespoon vegetable oil
· ½ cup chopped onions
· ½ cup chopped celery
· 3 sprigs of fresh thyme
· Turkey neck, cut into 4 pieces
· 4 cups turkey or chicken stock
· Pan drippings (about 1 to 2 cups)
· ¼ cup water, white wine or port wine
· 3 tablespoons cornstarch
· Salt and freshly cracked black pepper

Instructions:

· While the turkey is roasting, heat a small sauce pan
  with oil over medium heat and add onions and celery.
  Cook, stirring for 5 minutes or until vegetables are
  translucent. Add the turkey neck and allow it to
  brown. Add the turkey or chicken stock and fresh
  thyme and simmer for 30 minutes. Strain and reserve
  the stock for finishing the gravy.
· Once the turkey has finished roasting, drain the pan
  drippings into a measuring cup and skim off and
  discard the fat. Pour 1 cup of the liquid back into the
  roasting pan and over medium heat scrape the bottom
  to loosen all of the roasted bits in the pan. Pour the
  pan drippings, the reserved stock and the additional
  drippings from the roasting pan into a medium
  saucepan and begin to cook on medium-high heat.
· Dissolve the cornstarch in water or wine and whisk
  into the hot liquid. Bring to a boil and cook for two
  minutes, continually stirring until the gravy is thick.
  Taste and season with salt and pepper as necessary.
  Strain the gravy through a sieve. Serve hot.

BROWNED SAGE BUTTER

Ingredients:

· 1 stick (4 ounces) unsalted butter
· 4 to 6 fresh sage leaves

Instructions:

· Melt the butter in a small saucepan over medium-low
  heat. Add the sage leaves and continue to cook until
  the butter develops a golden color and a nutty aroma,
  about 15 to 20 minutes. Remove from the heat.

CHESTNUT DRESSING

serves 10

Ingredients:

- 8 tablespoons unsalted butter
- 8 ribs celery, chopped (3 cups)
- 2 medium yellow onions, chopped (3 cups)
- 4 small leeks, white part only, washed thoroughly, and then chopped (2 cups)
- ½ pound bulk pork or turkey sausage, cooked, drained and crumbled
- 1 cup coarsely chopped flat-leaf parsley
- 2 teaspoons fresh sage leaves, minced, or 1 teaspoon dried
- 2 teaspoons fresh thyme leaves, minced or 1 teaspoon dried
- 8 cups cubed dried Italian or sourdough bread (approximately 1 inch, crust left on)
- 3 to 4 cups turkey or chicken stock (see Note)
- 2 cups roasted whole chestnuts, broken into chunks
- Salt and freshly cracked black pepper, to taste

Instructions:

- Preheat oven to 350°F. Mist a 2-quart casserole with vegetable oil spray.
- Melt the butter in a large skillet over medium-high heat. Add the celery, onions and leeks and sauté for 4 to 5 minutes or until the vegetables are soft. Remove from the heat.
- In a large mixing bowl, mix together the cooked vegetables with the remaining ingredients, seasoning to taste. Allow the dressing to rest for 15 to 20 minutes to soak in the stock, mix again. Transfer the dressing to the prepared casserole and cover.
  (The dressing may be prepared to this point 1 day in advance and refrigerated. Add 15 to 20 minutes to the baking time since the dressing will be cold.)
- Bake, covered, for 30 minutes. Remove the cover and bake an additional 35 to 45 minutes. The top of the dressing should have a golden brown crust.

Note: Use the larger amount of stock if you prefer a more moist, soft-textured dressing. Less stock will produce a crisper dressing.

serves 10

Potato Ingredients:
- 4 pounds sweet potatoes (5 large potatoes)
- ½ cup heavy cream
- 4 tablespoons unsalted butter
- ¼ cup maple syrup
- ½ teaspoon salt

Topping Ingredients:
- 2 cups fresh breadcrumbs (3 slices of bread)
- 4 tablespoons unsalted butter, melted
- ½ cup light brown sugar
- ½ cup coarsely chopped pecans

Instructions:
- Preheat oven to 400°F.
- Prick the potatoes with a fork and place on a foil-lined tray. Roast for 60 minutes or until very tender.
- Remove the potatoes from the oven and cool slightly. Peel and discard the skin.
- Place the potatoes in a bowl and add the cream, butter, maple syrup and salt. Whip until very smooth.
- Butter a 2-quart casserole dish and fill with the potato mixture.
- For the topping, combine all of the ingredients and sprinkle over the potatoes.
- Bake at 350°F for 30 minutes. Check after 20 minutes; cover loosely with foil if the topping browns too quickly.

Note: The potatoes may be assembled 1 day in advance. Before baking, bring the casserole out of the refrigerator for 30 minutes. Cover and bake for 40 minutes at 350°F; uncover and bake for an additional 10 to 15 minutes for a total of 50 to 55 minutes.

GREEN BEANS WITH SHIITAKE MUSHROOMS

serves 10

Ingredients:
- 2½ to 3 pounds fresh green beans, trimmed
- 3 tablespoons unsalted butter
- 2 large shallots, minced or ½ cup minced red onion
- 1 pound fresh shiitake mushrooms, stems discarded, caps quartered
- ½ cup chicken or vegetable stock
- Salt and freshly cracked black pepper, to taste

Instructions:
- Bring a large pot of water to a boil, add the green beans and cook for 5 to 6 minutes (depending on the thickness of the beans) until they are slightly tender and bright green. Drain, rinse in cold water to cool, and drain again. (This step may be done 1 day in advance. Wrap the beans in damp paper towels, tuck inside a plastic bag, and refrigerate.)
- Melt the butter in a large, non-stick skillet over medium-high heat. Add the shallots and sauté for 2 minutes or until translucent. Add the mushrooms and cook for 2 minutes or until they start to wilt. Add the cooked green beans and pour in the stock. Gently toss to combine and season with salt and pepper. Sauté until the beans are heated through, about 5 to 7 minutes. Serve immediately.

ZESTY ORANGE CRANBERRY SAUCE

makes 4 cups

Ingredients:
- 1 pound fresh or frozen cranberries
- ¼ cup orange marmalade
- ½ cup cranberry juice
- ¼ cup freshly squeezed tangerine juice (about 3 tangerines) or orange juice (about 2 large oranges)
- ¾ cup granulated sugar
- 2 cinnamon sticks
- 2 oranges, peeled and sectioned
- ½ cup pomegranate seeds, optional

Instructions:
- Place all of the ingredients except the orange sections and optional pomegranate seeds in a medium saucepan and cook over medium heat for 12 to 15 minutes or until the sauce thickens and the cranberries pop.
- Remove the cinnamon sticks. Cool the sauce and fold in the orange sections and optional pomegranate seeds, cover and refrigerate. Cranberry sauce may be prepared several days in advance.

PIE DOUGH

makes one crust

Ingredients:

- 1¼ cups all-purpose flour
- Pinch of salt
- 6 tablespoons unsalted butter, cold and cut into 6 pieces
- 4 tablespoons shortening, cold
- 3 to 4 tablespoons ice cold water

Instructions:

- Combine flour and salt in a bowl or in a food processor and quickly blend together.
- Add the butter and shortening and cut it into the flour with two forks or pulse in the processor until the mixture has the texture of oatmeal with small bits of butter.
- Drizzle the water evenly over the mixture and combine or pulse until the dough barely comes together to form a ball. Do not overwork the dough. Empty the dough onto a large sheet of plastic wrap; use the wrap to shape the dough into a solid, flat disk.
- Seal the dough and chill for at least 30 minutes. The dough may be stored for 2 days in the refrigerator or for 1 month in the freezer.

APPLE BLACKBERRY CRUMBLE PIE

makes one 9-inch pie

Ingredients:

- 1 recipe Pie Dough
- 5 medium apples, 3 Granny Smith and 2 Golden Delicious, peeled, cored and cut into slices (7 cups)
- 2 cups blackberries, fresh or frozen
- 3 tablespoons all-purpose flour
- ½ cup granulated sugar
- ½ teaspoon cinnamon
- 1 recipe Streusel Topping

Instructions:

- On a lightly floured surface, roll out the pie dough to form a 12-inch circle.
- Lightly mist a 9-inch pie plate with vegetable oil spray and line with the dough. Trim and crimp the edges of the dough. Chill the pie shell for 30 minutes.
- Preheat oven to 425°F.
- Toss the apples, blackberries, flour, sugar and cinnamon in a large mixing bowl.
- Fill shell with the fruit and cover with the streusel topping.
- Bake for 30 minutes. Remove the pie and lower the temperature to 375°F. Loosely cover the pie with aluminum foil and bake for an additional 30 minutes or until the pie's juices are bubbling and thick.
- Cool the pie on a rack. Serve at room temperature.

STREUSEL TOPPING

Ingredients:

- 6 tablespoons light brown sugar
- 2 tablespoons granulated sugar
- ¾ cup all-purpose flour
- 1 teaspoon ground cinnamon
- 6 tablespoons unsalted butter, cold and cut into bits

Instructions:

- Place the first four ingredients together in a mixing bowl. Cut in the cold butter with two forks until the mixture looks crumbly. (You may also use a food processor outfitted with a steel blade, pulsing to create the desired texture.) Finish by pressing the mixture together in your hands to form coin-size clumps.

RACHEL'S FAVORITE PUMPKIN PIE

makes two 9-inch pies

Ingredients:
- 4 large eggs
- 1½ cups granulated sugar
- 1 teaspoon salt
- 2 teaspoons ground cinnamon
- 1 teaspoon ground nutmeg
- ½ teaspoon ground cloves
- 1 teaspoon ground ginger
- One 29-ounce can pumpkin puree
- Two 12-ounce cans evaporated milk
- 2 unbaked 9-inch pie shells, (4-cup volume)

Instructions:
- Preheat oven to 425°F.
- Beat the eggs in a large mixing bowl and quickly whisk in the sugar. Add the salt, cinnamon, nutmeg, cloves and ginger and mix to combine. Add the pumpkin and evaporated milk and whisk until smooth. Pour half of the pumpkin filling into each pie shell.
- Bake the pies for 15 minutes at 425°F. Lower the heat to 350°F and bake for an additional 40 to 50 minutes or until a toothpick inserted into the center of the pie comes out clean. Cool and serve with whipped cream.

· GOOD IDEA ·

If you are making your own pie dough, small cookies can be cut out of any remaining dough and baked. Garnish the finished pie with the small cookies.

· Pie Equals Love ·

J.W. Longaberger was famous for his handwoven baskets. His wife, Grandma Bonnie Longaberger is famous for her homemade pies. While raising her twelve children, she made a point to make dessert every day, and often that meant pies. Usually she baked three or four at a time and, always resourceful, cut each pie into fourths to eliminate requests for second helpings. "My son Rich was grown and left home before he realized other people didn't cut pies that way." Grandma Bonnie recalls.

ANYTIME AT ALL

SOME OF OUR FAVORITE GET-TOGETHERS HAVE NOTHING
TO DO WITH THE TIME OF YEAR, AND EVERYTHING TO DO
WITH THE PEOPLE WE CARE ABOUT. WE ALSO LOVE FINDING
CREATIVE WAYS TO SHOW JUST HOW MUCH WE CARE, WHICH
EXPLAINS WHY WE SOMETIMES FIND OURSELVES PITCHING
SAFARI TENTS IN OUR LIVING ROOMS, DANCING WITH SOM-
BREROS ON OUR HEADS, AND TYING UP STACKS OF COOKIES
WITH CUTE LITTLE BOWS. WHAT WILL YOU DO TO SHOW
HOW MUCH YOU CARE?

·IT'S A ZOO BIRTHDAY·
Party

AT THIS BIRTHDAY PARTY, THINGS GET A LITTLE WILD, BUT EVERYONE HAS A ROARING GOOD TIME!

It's hard to say who's going to have more fun with this party—you or your little animal-lover. Start by gathering all your houseplants in the party room to create an instant jungle. Wrap a grass skirt around the party table. Pitch a tent and pass around the pith helmets. If you really want to go all out, add camp chairs, a hammock and mosquito netting.

· recipes ·

SPEARED HAM *and* CHEESE CHUNKS
CRISPY CRITTER DRUMSTICKS
ANTS ON A LOG
NUTS *and* BERRIES TRAIL MIX
CUPCAKES *with* SHORTBREAD COOKIE TOPPERS

· projects ·

JUNGLE LEAF INVITATIONS
PARTY ANIMAL BAGS
JUNGLE TABLE
SLITHERING SNAKE PARTY FAVORS

· getting started ·

· PLANNING TIPS ·

- On invitations, ask guests to RSVP by a certain date, preferably one week before the party. The more accurate your head count, the less you'll have to guess when purchasing party goods.

- Parents sometimes ask for gift ideas when they call to RSVP, so have a few in mind.

- Don't forget to pick up a box of thank-you notes. Or cut out extra leaves when making Jungle Leaf invitations, and the birthday boy or girl can write a short thank-you note on each leaf.

- Have a few extra party favors on hand, just in case guests show up with a little brother or sister in tow.

· TO DO LIST ·

- **3 Weeks Before:**
  Compile guest list.
  Make and send out Jungle Leaf Invitations.
  Order pith helmets.
  Begin gathering decorations and prizes.

- **2 Weeks Before:**
  Bake and freeze cupcakes.
  Make Slithering Snake Party Favors.

- **1 Week Before:**
  Make party bags and fill with goodies.
  Decorate party cups.
  Make jungle leaf place mats.

- **2-3 Days Before:**
  Purchase groceries.
  Make Nuts and Berries Trail Mix.

- **Day Before:**
  Begin to set up decorations and props.
  Defrost cupcakes.
  Make and refrigerate Speared Ham and Cheese Chunks.
  Make Shortbread Cookie Toppers.

- **Party Day:**
  Finish decorating.
  Assemble Jungle Table.
  Prepare Crispy Critter Drumsticks.
  Decorate cupcakes.
  Assemble pineapple tree.
  Assemble Ants On A Log and refrigerate.

JUNGLE LEAF INVITATIONS

SUPPLIES

for each:

One 5x7-inch natural
craft paper envelope

One 5x7-inch sheet of
heavy craft paper

Two 5x7-inch sheets green
construction paper

Markers in jungle colors

Brass butterfly brad

Hole punch

Scissors

Glue stick, optional

1. Stack the three pieces of paper and cut into a basic leaf shape. Punch a hole through all three where the stem would be.

2. With scissors, fringe the edges of the 2 green leaves as illustrated.

3. At the top of the craft paper, draw or glue on a picture of a zoo animal. Fill in the party information with a marker.

4. Attach the three paper leaves with the brass butterfly brad. Place in envelope, seal and address.

• VARIATION •

Here's an easy and inexpensive alternate invitation idea: Color-copy a favorite photo of your child onto card stock paper and cut to the size of a standard invitation envelope. Draw a pith helmet on his or her head with a marker, and write the party information next to the picture. Decorate the envelopes with brightly colored animal stickers and mail.

SUPPLIES

for each:

Brown paper lunch bag
Green construction paper
Natural raffia
Acrylic paint
(we used black, white and golden brown)
#6 paintbrush
Black marker
Pinking shears
Scissors
Hole punch
Animal print stamp, optional
Goodies to fill

1. Fold the top of the lunch bag down 2 inches. Trim with pinking shears and punch 2 holes horizontally. You will be painting the front surface only. The top will stay folded.

2. For the leopard print bag, paint a swath of golden brown down the left and right side. Paint a band of white down the middle. Blend together at the edges. Dry. With the black paint and #6 brush, paint on broken circles to make leopard spots. Or use an animal print stamp available at craft stores.

3. For the zebra print bag, paint wide black stripes down the front of the lunch bag as illustrated.

4. For the name tag, cut a 4-inch leaf from green construction paper. Fringe the edges with scissors, and punch a hole through one end. Add the child's name with black marker.

5. Fill the bag with goodies. Thread the raffia through the holes in the bag, then through the hole in the leaf. Tie with a bow.

What's in the Bag?

Box of raisins or animal crackers
Plastic jungle animals
Barrel of Monkeys
Animal print pencils
Compass
Small canteen
Animal stickers

HOW TO CREATE YOUR PARTY TABLE:

1. Start with a tablecloth made of burlap or other inexpensive fabric. Rolls of burlap are available inexpensively at garden supply stores.

2. Use safety pins to pin the grass skirt to the burlap. Grass skirts can be found at party supply stores and are available in a variety of sizes and colors. Be sure to measure your table before purchasing.

3. For place mats, cut giant leaf shapes out of the green construction paper. Use the full length of paper for each leaf.

4. Paint white paper cups using the same techniques as for the Party Animal Bags (page 158). For the leopard print, paint the outside of the cup golden brown. (You can try watering the golden brown down a bit to achieve leopard-like color variations.) With black paint and a #6 brush, paint on broken circles for leopard spots. For the zebra print, paint the same wide black stripes as shown for the lunch bag. Let dry and fill with jungle juice!

· GOOD IDEA ·

Pith helmets are so much cooler than party hats, plus they're inexpensive when purchased from an online party store. If you're too short on time to make our Slithering Snake Party Favors, the same online stores carry toy binoculars and mini compasses. No time to decorate party cups with animal prints? Order plastic canteens! Place your order three weeks ahead of time, if possible, to allow plenty of time for shipping.

SUPPLIES

for each:

One slightly used
necktie

Two 4-inch x 5-foot
strips of polyester
quilting batting

One 5-foot length of
16-gauge wire

Red felt, for the tongue

Assorted felt scraps,
for the eyes

2 buttons, for the eyes

Needle

Thread

Scissors

*We suggest that an adult
make these adorable party
gifts prior to party time.*

1. With scissors, cut open the necktie to reveal the lining and interfacing.

2. Without stitching through the lining, sew on snake eyes by layering felt scraps with buttons. Cut a long forked tongue (ours is about 5 inches long) from the red felt. Tack it with thread under the large point of the necktie. Set aside.

3. Bend one end of the wire to conform to the diamond shape of the necktie face. Twist to secure. Then twist a loop at the other end for the tail.

4. Wrap the batting strips around the length of wire. Wrap the thread around the batting in the same manner. Knot the thread on both ends to secure.

5. Insert the wrapped wire in between the lining and interfacing at both ends.

6. Stitch closed.

7. Coil your Slithering Snake, or slither it through a house plant.

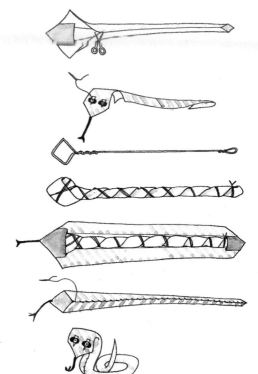

· They Ate The Cake. Now What? ·

Never underestimate the number of party activities kids this age can go through. To make sure you don't end up with half an hour of nothing-to-do party time during which guests start acting like, well, animals, plan one more activity than you think you'll need. Like:

· Pin The Tail On The Tiger.

· Safari Hunt (Hide small toy jungle animals in easy-to-find places.)

· Animal-Face Face Painting (Look for easy how-tos on the Internet.)

· Tarzan-Yelling Contest (You might want to do this one outdoors.)

· Guess How Many? (Guests guess how many animal crackers are inside a glass jar. Winner takes all.)

Be sure to provide a kid-friendly environment by removing any breakables or other objects that could cause bumps and bruises when playing the games below.

SNAKES ALIVE!

Create an obstacle course from packing boxes, tables, chair cushions and whatever else you can find. Time how long it takes for each guest to slither through the "snake trail." Everyone who plays wins a Slithering Snake Party Favor!

GIANT SPIDER WEB

For each guest, tie a small prize to a ball of yarn or string. For the prize shown, we bought take-out food containers, made a few cuts on one side, and decorated them to look like a cage. Inside? A "wild" bean-bag animal! Hide the prize, then wrap the string over and around multiple objects in the room until you've worked your way to the door. Repeat with each prize and ball of yarn. When you're done, you'll have created a room-size web. Each guest chooses a ball of yarn by the door and follows it through the maze, rewinding the ball as they climb over and under the other guests' strings to find their prize. Weave a fairly simple web, especially for kids under 6.

WHAT'S THAT SOUND?

Remember the tent you pitched for a party decoration? Make it do double duty by turning it into a game. Here's how: Two kids go in and the rest stand outside near the tent. One guest on the outside makes an animal noise and the two kids inside the tent have to guess not only what animal sound it is, but who is making it!

SPEARED HAM AND CHEESE CHUNKS

Ingredients and Materials:
- Wooden Popsicle sticks
- High quality baked ham cut into 1 to 1½-inch squares
- Roasted turkey breast cut into 1 to 1½-inch squares
- Mild and white cheddar cheese cut into 1 to 1½-inch squares
- 1 whole large pineapple
- Carrot threads or peels

Instructions:
- Thread 3 to 4 cubes of meat and cheese onto each stick. Pierce the pineapple with a paring knife to start a hole for each stick. Force each stick into the pineapple. Place the skewer-filled pineapple on a plate or in a shallow bowl and surround it with carrot threads or peels.

> · **GOOD TO KNOW** ·
>
> Make a snack that's healthy and zoo-friendly, too: Make a Banana Boat! Just place a few bunches of perfectly ripened bananas in Longaberger's Row Your Boat™ Basket, then add a stuffed monkey for good measure. The kids will go ape, and their moms will think you're the cat's meow!

· recipes ·

CRISPY CRITTER DRUMSTICKS

makes 8 pieces

Ingredients:
- 8 small chicken legs
- 2 cups buttermilk
- Salt and pepper
- 2 large eggs, lightly beaten
- ½ cup all-purpose flour
- 1 cup Panko Japanese style bread crumbs, available at Asian food markets
- Vegetable oil for frying

Instructions:
- Rinse the chicken well and place in a shallow dish. Season with salt and pepper. Pour the buttermilk over the legs, cover with plastic wrap and refrigerate for 4 hours or overnight.
- Remove the chicken from the buttermilk and pat dry.
- Pour oil, at least 2 inches deep, into a large, heavy-bottomed frying pan; heat oil to 350°F.
- Preheat oven to 350°F.
- Assemble three shallow dishes and fill one each with eggs, flour and bread crumbs. Dip each leg first into the flour, then into the egg mixture and finally roll in the bread crumbs. Transfer each piece to a tray.
- Cook the drumsticks in batches in the hot oil until brown on each side, about 4 to 5 minutes total time. Transfer the browned chicken to a baking sheet fitted with a rack. Bake in the 350°F oven for 12 to 15 minutes or until the juices run clear. Serve hot or cold with dipping sauces such as, barbeque sauce, honey mustard, salsa, blue cheese dip, ranch dressing or apricot mustard sauce.

Ingredients:
- Celery, rinsed
- Peanut butter
- Raisins
- Golden raisins (a moister, plumper raisin)
- Cocktail peanuts

Instructions:
- Cut the celery stalks into 4-inch sticks. Fill a pastry bag fitted with a pastry tip with peanut butter. Fill the center of each piece of celery with peanut butter. Top each with a sprinkling of raisins and peanuts. Place on a tray lined with parchment or wax paper, cover and refrigerate until ready to serve. These may be prepared several hours before serving.

makes 10 cups

Ingredients:
- 1 cup honey roasted peanuts
- 1 cup dried cranberries
- 1 cup mixed, dried fruit bits
- 1 cup banana chips
- 2 cups dried pineapple chunks
- 2 cups sweetened puffed wheat cereal
- 2 cups animal crackers

Instructions:
- Gently toss all ingredients together in a large bowl. Store in an airtight container. Trail Mix may be made several days in advance.

Ingredients and Materials:

- Favorite flavor ice cream
- Frosted cupcakes, paper liners removed
- Shortbread Cookie Toppers: see page 182 for shortbread recipe.
- Icing in jungle colors, for cookie toppers
- Birthday candles

Instructions:

- Frost cookie toppers.
- Place 1 or 2 scoops of ice cream into each mug. Carefully position the frosted cupcake on top of the ice cream. Press the iced cookie topper(s) into the frosting of the cupcake. Add birthday candles to one or all of the cupcakes.

· **GOOD IDEA** ·

No time to make the shortbread toppers? Use packaged animal crackers or cut-out cookies from your favorite bakery.

RED HOT BIRTHDAY

· Fiesta! ·

THIS FESTIVE PARTY IS ALL ABOUT FLAVORFUL FOODS GUESTS CAN ASSEMBLE THEMSELVES.

Start with bright colors borrowed from south of the border. String up a canvas canopy, cantina lights and surprise-filled piñatas. Turn simple chili peppers into the hottest decorations around. Scatter vases of sunny gerbera daisies here and there. Sling sombreros on chair backs and throw one on the floor, in case anyone's in the mood for a hat dance. Now all that's left to do is stand back and shout "Olé!"

· recipes ·

SANTA FE SALAD
OLÉ! RICE
SPICY CHICKEN TACOS
ICE CREAM SUNDAE STATION
DEVIL'S FOOD CAKE

· projects ·

CHILI PEPPER INVITATIONS
FIESTA PLACE CARDS
HANDCRAFTED PIÑATAS

· getting started ·

· PLANNING TIPS ·

- Devil's Food Cake layers may be baked and frozen ahead of time. Defrost the layers the day before the party, then immediately assemble and frost the cake to seal in freshness and moistness.

- If you're planning this party for teenagers, plan for nonstop music and extra activities like conversation starting games or a karaoke machine. And don't worry about videotaping a teen's party - they'll have a great time doing it themselves!

- Plan to have everything ready for the party one hour before the guests are due to arrive. That leaves time to shower and dress without rushing.

TO DO LIST

- **3 Weeks Before:**
  Compile guest list.
  Make and send out Chili Pepper Invitations.
  Begin gathering decorations.

- **Two Weeks Before:**
  Make Handcrafted Piñatas.

- **One Week Before:**
  Bake and freeze Devil's Food Cake layers.

- **2-3 Days Before:**
  Purchase groceries.

- **Day Before:**
  Defrost cake and frost.
  Set party table and put up decorations.
  Set up table for Ice Cream Sundae Station.
  Make Fiesta Place Cards.
  Prepare chicken for tacos.
  Prepare Creamy Southwestern Dressing.

- **Party Day:**
  Assemble Santa Fe Salad but do not toss with dressing until just before serving.
  Prepare Olé! Rice.
  Prepare sundae ingredients.
  Have a red-hot good time!

CHILI PEPPER INVITATIONS

SUPPLIES

for each:

One brightly colored
5x7-inch envelope

One 8-1/2x11-inch sheet
natural cover stock paper,
for taco shell

One 4-1/4x6-1/2-inch sheet
red cover stock paper,
for the chili pepper

One 2-inch square bright
green cover stock paper,
for the stem

Acrylic paints
(we used white, yellow
and turquoise)

Green tissue paper,
for lettuce

Brightly colored markers

Gel pens, optional

#3 round paintbrush

Scissors

Glue stick

1. Fold the natural paper in half. With scissors, trim to fit the envelope then round the unfolded corners to resemble a taco shell.

2. Cut a chili pepper shape from the red paper. For the stem, cut a star, about 1½-inch diameter, from the green paper. Glue the stem onto the chili pepper.

3. On one side of the chili pepper, fill in your party information with acrylic paint or gel pens.

4. Cut a few thin strips of green tissue paper for lettuce. Place the lettuce and chili pepper inside the taco shell and slide into the envelope. Address your invitations with the brightly colored markers.

· GOOD IDEA ·

Wrap jars of delicious salsas in brightly colored tissue paper for easy party favors that your guests can savor later. For a special treat, give them our best-selling Peach Salsa from Longaberger Homestead.® Call our Personal Shopper Line at 1-740-322-5588, option 2, and the friendly folks there will gladly ship your order.

FIESTA PLACE CARDS

SUPPLIES
for each:

5 assorted hot peppers
1 craft tag
2 strands of raffia
Brightly colored markers
Fishing line
Large-eye needle

1. With the fishing line and needle, thread together the 5 peppers as illustrated. Knot the fishing line, and tie into a bundle. Be sure to wash your hands right away, because the oil in hot peppers is an irritant.

2. Write your guest's name on the craft tag.

3. With the raffia, tie the pepper bundle and tag together with a bow.

· Kaitlin's Sweet 16 ·

When Rachel Longaberger's daughter, Kaitlin, turned 16, she celebrated with friends and family at a downtown Columbus, Ohio, restaurant known for its fabulous food and funky atmosphere. Her party brought back memories of other birthday parties, including a formal children's tea party when she was just a little girl, which featured frilly dresses and afternoon tea. Although Kaitlin's parties have varied as she's grown older, some things never change - Longaberger birthdays are always focused on family, friends and fond memories in the making.

SUPPLIES

for each:

One large balloon and one small balloon
Masking tape and duct tape
Newspaper
Papier-mâché paste (available at art supply stores)
Airtight container
Empty coffee can
Plastic sheeting to cover work surfaces
Two florist wire hoops
Assorted colors of tissue paper
Assorted colors of construction paper
White glue
Scissors and hobby knife
Small candies and novelties to fill the piñata

1. Because piñatas take considerable drying time, plan to make them at least a week before your party. Cover your work area with sheets of plastic. Inflate the large and small balloons. With masking tape, gently tape the balloons together to create the shape of a bird. Use the coffee can as a stand.

2. Cut or tear the newspaper into 2x6-inch strips. Mix the papier-mâché paste in the airtight container according to the package instructions. Coat a strip of newspaper with the paste and smooth it onto the surface of your balloon bird. Repeat until the bird is completely covered by 4 layers of newspaper. Let dry overnight. Repeat this process until your piñata has at least 12 layers. If you plan on filling it with lots of candy, you'll need to add extra layers.

3. Once your bird is completely dry, cut a small hole in its back (the balloon will pop). Partially fill with candy and novelties. Poke 2 florist wire hoops through the back body of the bird and secure on the inside with duct tape. Tape the hole closed with masking tape.

4. Roll 3 sheets of tissue paper (all the same color) together. Cut the roll into 3-inch wide sections. Cut each section into feather shapes, as shown, leaving about 1 inch at the top to glue onto the bird body. Unroll.

5. Working from the bottom up, squeeze a line of glue around the body of the bird. Gently press on a feather strip. The next glue line should be about 1 inch above the previously glued strip so that the feathers overlap. Continue layering, changing colors as needed. Keep the hanging hoops free of tissue paper. Let dry for several hours.

6. For the wings, tail and beak, cut shapes from brightly colored construction paper. Fold for extra dimension, if desired. Glue into place. Hang, and let the games begin!

SANTA FE SALAD

serves 10 *to* 12

Ingredients:

- 8 to 10 cups torn Romaine lettuce
- 1 small red onion, cut in half then cut into thin slices
- 1 cup fresh corn kernels, blanched for 1 minute then cooled
- 2 celery ribs, sliced (about 1 cup)
- 1 cup cooked garbanzo beans
- 1 small jicama, peeled and cut into matchsticks
- 3 beefsteak tomatoes, cut into 6 wedges
- 1 recipe Creamy Southwestern Dressing

Instructions:

- Place the lettuce in a large bowl. Sprinkle with onion, corn, celery, beans and jicama. Gently toss. Randomly tuck tomato wedges into the salad. Serve individual portions with a drizzling of Creamy Southwestern Dressing.

CREAMY SOUTHWESTERN DRESSING

makes 1 ¼ *cups*

Ingredients:

- ½ cup favorite salsa (mild, medium or hot)
- Juice of ½ lime
- 2 minced scallions, white parts only
- 1 garlic clove, minced
- ½ cup extra-virgin olive oil
- ¼ cup sour cream
- Sea salt and freshly cracked black pepper
- 2 tablespoons chopped fresh cilantro

Instructions:

- In a blender, combine all ingredients except the cilantro. Blend for 30 seconds. Stir in the cilantro and add salt and pepper, to taste. Store in an airtight container in the refrigerator. The dressing may be made one day in advance.

· GOOD TO KNOW ·

Here are two ways to make your Fiesta a hit with Longaberger Pottery® and Baskets® working together:

· An unheated Woven Traditions® 1-Quart Covered Casserole rests beautifully in the protector of a 9" Bowl Basket for festive serving anytime.

· To keep flour tortillas warm gather together a Darning Basket, two Woven Traditions® Luncheon Plates and a Woven Traditions® 2-Quart Casserole Lid. First, warm the Luncheon Plates in a low oven. While warm, place one Luncheon Plate upside-down in the basket. Place the second Luncheon Plate right side up on top of the first plate. The Luncheon Plates will be bottom to bottom in the basket. Place your warm flour tortillas on top of the warm Luncheon Plates and cover with the 2-Quart Casserole Lid. Now your flour tortillas will stay warm longer!

• recipes •

serves 10 *to* 12

Ingredients:
- 2 tablespoons vegetable oil
- 1 small onion, diced (½ cup)
- One 4-ounce can chopped green chilies, drained
- 2 cups white rice
- 4 cups chicken or vegetable stock
- Sea salt and freshly ground pepper
- One 16-ounce can black beans, rinsed and drained
- ½ cup chopped fresh cilantro
- ¼ cup chopped fresh parsley
- Juice of 1 lime

Instructions:
- Heat the oil in a medium saucepan over medium-high heat. Add the onions and chilies and sauté for 3 to 5 minutes or until the onions are translucent.
- Add the rice and sauté for 3 more minutes. Pour in the chicken stock and a pinch each of salt and pepper. Bring to a boil, then reduce the heat and cover with a lid. Cook for 20 minutes or until all of the stock is absorbed.
- Add the beans, cilantro, parsley and lime juice and gently toss. Add salt and pepper, to taste. Fluff with a fork and serve.

SPICY CHICKEN TACOS

serves 10 *to* 12

Ingredients:
- 5 to 6 pounds chicken breasts with bones and skin
- 1 large onion, sliced into 8 pieces
- 2 garlic cloves, crushed
- 2 bay leaves
- 2 cinnamon sticks
- 1 teaspoon sea salt
- 2 teaspoons ground cumin
- 1 tablespoon chili powder
- ¼ teaspoon cayenne pepper
- Two 10-ounce cans tomatoes with green chilies
- Two 10-ounce cans enchilada sauce
- 12 taco shells

Instructions:
- Combine all ingredients, except the taco shells, in a large heavy-bottomed pot. Add 1 cup of water and bring to a boil. Reduce the heat to low, cover with a lid and cook for 20 to 25 minutes or until the breasts are cooked, but not dry. Remove the chicken from the liquid.
- Increase the heat to high and reduce the liquid in the pot to 3½ cups of liquid.
- Remove and discard the chicken skin and bones from the cooked breasts. Shred the chicken meat.
- Strain the reduced liquid, and let it rest for several minutes. Skim and discard any fat that rises to the top of the surface.
- Return the sauce to the pan, add the shredded meat and reheat. The chicken filling may be prepared up to 1 day in advance and stored, covered, in the refrigerator.
- Serve with warmed taco shells, shredded lettuce, diced tomatoes, shredded cheese, sour cream and salsa.

ICE CREAM SUNDAE STATION

Ingredients:

- 2-3 flavors of ice cream
- Ice cream sauces (we used caramel nut, chocolate and butterscotch)
- Ice cream toppings such as nuts, colored sprinkles, toasted coconut and cherries with stems
- Whipped cream
- Additional ingredients as desired: cones, fresh fruit sauces, marshmallow or hot fudge sauce, fresh berries, crushed chocolate cookies, diced pound cake and assorted candy bits

Instructions:

- Be sure your selection of sauces complements the ice cream flavor, and offer a variety of toppings to please any palate.
- Create your sundae station on a serving area with plenty of room for sundae-makers to mingle while creating their delicious concoctions.

· GOOD TO KNOW ·

A round half-gallon container of ice cream fits perfectly in our 2-quart Pickling™ Crock. Place the crock in the freezer for an hour before serving; then simply place the container of ice cream right inside the ice cold crock and it will stay frozen longer.

· GOOD IDEA ·

Add a warm glow to your table with these colorful pepper votive holders.

1. Hollow out the pepper as you would a pumpkin. Remove and discard the seeds, spines and top of the pepper. Cut through the bottom so the pepper fits over a votive candle and rests securely on a flat, burn-safe surface.

2. With a hobby knife, carve patterns into the sides of the pepper. Try stars, circles, letters or flowers.

3. Wrap the votive candle in a small square of aluminum foil to catch any melted wax and place on a flat, burn-safe surface. Top votive candle with the carved pepper and light. Muy Bonita!

DEVIL'S FOOD CAKE

serves 10 to 12

Ingredients:
- ½ cup Dutch process cocoa
- 2½ cups cake flour
- ¼ teaspoon salt
- 1½ teaspoons baking soda
- 1¼ cups granulated sugar
- ½ cup loosely packed light brown sugar
- 3 large eggs, room temperature
- 1 cup sour cream, room temperature
- 1 cup (2 sticks) unsalted butter, room temperature, cut into ½-inch pieces
- 1 recipe Buttercream Frosting

Instructions:
- Preheat oven to 350°F. Butter and line two 9-inch round pans with parchment paper.
- Combine the cocoa with ½ cup boiling water in a small bowl and mix well. Set aside to cool.
- Combine the flour, salt, baking soda and both sugars in the bowl of an electric mixer. Mix on low for 30 seconds or until the ingredients are completely combined.
- Whisk together the eggs and sour cream in a bowl. Add half of the egg mixture and the butter to the dry ingredients and mix for 1 minute. The batter should be moist and thick. Add the remaining egg and cocoa mixture and mix on medium-high speed for 1 minute. Scrape the sides of the bowl and mix for an additional 1 minute.
- Divide the batter evenly between the prepared pans and bake for 25 to 30 minutes or until a toothpick inserted into the center of each cake comes out clean.
- Transfer the cakes to cooling racks. After 5 minutes invert the pans, remove the cakes and allow them to cool completely.
- To assemble the cake, slice off the rounded tops of each layer to create a flat surface. Using a metal

spatula, generously frost the top of one layer, then place the other layer on top of it. Spread a thin coat of frosting on the top and sides of the cake, sealing in all of the crumbs. Apply a second, more generous layer of frosting to the sides and top of the cake swirling the frosting to create a finished look.

BUTTER CREAM FROSTING

makes 4 cups

Ingredients:
- 1 cup (2 sticks) unsalted butter, room temperature
- 7 cups confectioners' sugar
- 1 tablespoon vanilla extract
- ¾ cup sour cream

Instructions:
- In the bowl of an electric mixer, cream the butter. Add the confectioners' sugar and mix on low speed for 2 minutes or until smooth. Add the vanilla and sour cream. Mix on medium high for 1 to 2 minutes until smooth.

GOODIES FOR A
Good Cause

THE KEYS TO A SUCCESSFUL BAKE SALE FUND-RAISER ARE GOOD PLANNING, PROMOTION AND PRESENTATION. WE SHOW YOU HOW TO DO ALL THREE.

Is there anything more American than a good, old-fashioned bake sale? It's probably the most widespread example of our tradition of working together toward a common goal, of creating a sense of community, and of sharing our love of sweets. Encourage kids to join the effort. They'll learn about pitching in to help a good cause, while reinforcing math skills by portioning cakes and counting change. Need another reason to have a bake sale? Organizers earn the right to take home any unclaimed leftovers!

We stocked our bake sale with the sweetest recipes from this book plus a few new favorites:

· recipes ·

OHIO BUCKEYES
SHORTBREAD COOKIES
CARAMEL BUBBLE BREAD
CITRUS SQUARES
WHOOPIE PIES

CHOCOLATE PECAN BARS, PAGE 139
CRANBERRY ORANGE NUT BREAD, PAGE 34
WHITE CHOCOLATE PECAN FUDGE, PAGE 33
OATMEAL APPLE TOFFEE DROPS, PAGE 56
CRYSTAL SNOWBALL COOKIES, PAGE 57
NUTTY CARAMEL APPLES, PAGE 128
BANANA CRUMB MUFFINS, PAGE 43
NUTS AND BERRIES TRAIL MIX, PAGE 164
DEVIL'S FOOD CAKE, PAGE 175

· projects ·

PRESENTABLE PRICE SIGNS
TREAT-WRAPPING TECHNIQUES

· getting started ·

· PLANNING TIPS ·

- Schedule your sale before, during or after another well-attended event, like a school play, basketball game or concert.

- Fridays are good days for bake sales too—post a sign that encourages customers to stock up on treats for the weekend.

- Place a large trash basket beside your sales table. Clip on a large "trash" label with a clothespin.

- Remind volunteer bakers to label any non-disposable containers with their names.

- Baked goods make people thirsty! To enhance your bottom line, why not also sell coffee, lemonade, fruit punch, apple cider or bottled water?

- Identify your sales team with special t-shirts, badges or aprons.

- Charge the same amount for everything and portion accordingly.

- After the sale, don't forget to take down all your flyers, and personally thank volunteers.

· TO DO LIST ·

- **3 Weeks Before:**
  Decide on a bake sale location and obtain permission to use it.

- **1-2 Weeks Before:**
  Solicit volunteer bakers. More bakers mean a greater selection of treats.
  Start promoting your sale by posting flyers around town.
  Provide volunteers with coordinated wrapping supplies.

- **Day Before:**
  Place the following in a Medium Market Basket to take to the sale:
  - o Small paper plates
  - o Bread knife for portioning
  - o Spatula
  - o Paper napkins
  - o A handful of one dollar bills and a roll of quarters for making change
  - o Sale and pricing signs
  - o Sandwich bags

  Also bring, if necessary, a cooler.

- **Sale Day:**
  Allow plenty of time to set up baked goods and signs. Count your profits!

EASY BAKE SALE BANNER

Cut large triangles out of heavy paper or poster board. Cut letters out of the same paper, alternating colors for both letters and triangles, and glue into place. Hang on a clothesline with clothespins.

PRIZE WINNING LOLLIPOPS

Add color and fun to your next bake sale with the Lollipop Game. Make a lollipop tree by sticking lollipops into a styrofoam cone. Place a mark on the bottom of about 10 percent of the lollipop sticks. Customers pay before they choose a lollipop, and if they choose one with a mark, they win a whole pie, cake or plate of baked goods!

PRESENTABLE PRICE SIGNS

SUPPLIES

Cover stock paper in your organization's colors

20-gauge silver jewelry wire

Lollipop sticks

Pinking shears

Scissors

Glue stick

Markers

Florist clay

Hole punch

For Baskets and Crocks:

Glue a 1½-inch square of cover stock paper onto a 2-inch square of cover stock paper with pinked edges. Punch 2 holes into the top. Curl jewelry wire through the holes leaving enough wire at the top for bending over the basket edges. Fill in price or product information with a marker.

For Wrought Iron Stands:

Make flags by gluing cover stock paper triangles onto lollipop sticks. Add your organization's logo with a marker and hold in place with florist clay.

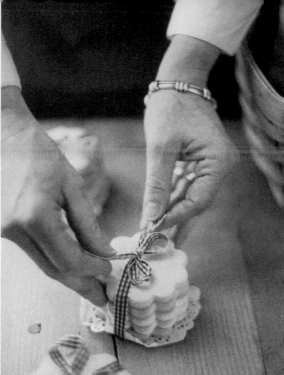

SUPPLY OPTIONS FOR WRAPPING:

Vellum envelopes
Wax paper
Rolls of cellophane
Gift bags
Nut cups
Candy boxes
Paper plates
Cover stock paper
Shipping tags
Key tags
Circle stickers
Square stickers
Ribbons and string
Rick rack
Toothpicks
Wooden skewers
Markers
Pinking shears
Scissors
Hole punch
Glue stick

WRAP IT UP IN WAX PAPER OR VELLUM:

- **Giant Cookies:** Use 4x6-inch vellum envelopes available at craft and printer-supply stores. Add a logo on a price sticker.
- **Whoopie Pies:** Seal a square vellum envelope, cut it on the diagonal with pinking shears, slip a pie into each half and then add a colorful string bow.
- **Snowball Cookies:** Roll 6 snowball cookies into a wax paper bag, tie with rick rack and finish with a square sticker.
- **Brownies and Quick Breads:** Wrap the old-fashioned way in neatly folded wax paper. Tie with a simple string and label with a sticker.

WRAP IT UP IN GIFT BAGS AND BOXES:

- **Trail Mix:** Scoop some into a gift bag; fold down the top of the bag. Use pinking shears to trim the edges. Punch a hole through the folds and tie with a bow. Label with key tags or plain stickers.
- **Fudge:** Embellish craft store candy boxes with wrap-around bands of pinked-edge paper and gingham bows. Dress up smaller boxes with a sticker and knotted ribbon.

WRAP IT UP IN CELLOPHANE:

- **Bar Cookies and Brownies:** Present on a rigid paper plate, generously wrapped in cellophane and tied with a gingham bow.
- **Ohio Buckeyes:** Place in solid-color nut cups, wrap in cellophane and tie with ribbon.
- **Caramel Apples:** Turn the sticks into flagpoles with glued-on paper pennants. Center each apple on a square of cellophane and tie all four corners onto the stick with a bow.
- **Muffins and Cupcakes:** Place a toothpick flag into each top.

• recipes •

OHIO BUCKEYES

makes 6 dozen buckeyes

Ingredients:
- 4 cups confectioners' sugar
- 1 cup graham cracker crumbs
- 1 cup coconut flakes
- 1 cup peanut butter
- 1 cup (2 sticks) unsalted butter, softened
- 8 ounces chocolate chips
- ½ bar paraffin wax, chopped into bits

Instructions:
- Line a tray with parchment or wax paper.
- Combine the sugar, crumbs, coconut, peanut butter and butter in a bowl. Mix thoroughly by hand or with a mixer. Form 1-inch balls and place on the prepared tray. Cover the tray and refrigerate 2 hours.
- Melt the chocolate chips and paraffin in the top of a double boiler over simmering water. Mix thoroughly.
- Poke each peanut butter ball with a wooden toothpick and dip into the warm chocolate, covering all but the top quarter of each ball. (The small circle of exposed peanut butter gives these treats the look of buckeye nuts.) Place each dipped buckeye on the lined tray. Chill to set the chocolate. Store in an airtight container in the refrigerator for up to 2 weeks.

• GOOD TO KNOW •

Boost traffic and profits by holding a drawing for a beautifully decorated layer cake displayed in a Longaberger Cake Basket. Winning the cake is grand, but winning the cake and the basket is the best prize of all!

• Welcome to Longaberger University •

Our bake sale was photographed at Longaberger University, an historic school building built back in 1876 in our hometown of Dresden, Ohio. Today, Longaberger University hosts training and education programs for Longaberger Consultants and employees. And, for two weeks every summer, the building houses a bereavement camp for children who have lost loved ones.

It's also the place where our founder, Dave Longaberger, repeated first grade twice and fifth grade three times. As a child, Dave struggled with epilepsy and was a severe stutterer, but that wasn't his explanation for his fifth grade troubles. "Back then I couldn't understand why my teacher, Ruby Adams, made me take fifth grade three times. Years later, I figured it out. She must have really liked me."

SHORTBREAD COOKIES

makes 2 dozen 2½-inch cookies

Ingredients:

- 2¼ cups all-purpose flour, plus extra for rolling
- ¼ cup cornstarch
- ½ teaspoon baking powder
- Pinch of salt
- ¾ cup confectioners' sugar
- 1 cup (2 sticks) unsalted butter, chilled and cut into ½-inch bits
- 1 large egg plus 1 large egg yolk
- 2 teaspoons vanilla extract

Instructions:

- Place flour, cornstarch, baking powder, salt and confectioner's sugar in a food processor. Pulse a few times to mix. Add the butter bits all at once and blend until the mixture resembles cornmeal.
- Combine the egg, egg yolk and vanilla in a small bowl. Add to the dry mix, pulsing the machine several times until the dough just comes together; do not over mix.
- Divide the dough into 2 pieces. Press each into a disk, wrap in plastic wrap and refrigerate for 1 hour. (The dough will freeze up to 1 month.)

- Preheat oven to 375°F.
- Remove the dough from the refrigerator and let it rest at room temperature for 10 minutes. Lightly dust your work surface with flour and roll dough out to about ¼ inch thick. Cut out desired shapes and transfer the cookies to ungreased cookie sheets. Bake 7 to 12 minutes. The edges of the cookies should be light golden brown.
- Allow the cookies to set for several minutes before transferring them to a cooling rack and cool completely.

· GOOD IDEA ·

Next time you're planning a neighborhood tag sale, why not plan a bake sale to go with it? Proceeds can go toward neighborhood improvements or a local cause. Older kids can operate the sale with minimal adult supervision. And customers will be delighted to take a break from bargain hunting to refuel on fresh-baked treats and just-brewed coffee.

· Chocolate Dipped Pretzel Sticks ·

These are easy and they go fast. To make them, generously spoon melted chocolate coating chips onto large pretzel rods, then immediately roll each rod in colored sprinkles. You could also dip rods in white chocolate coating chips, and roll in chocolate sprinkles. A 12-ounce bag of coating chips yields 12 well-coated pretzels. Don't they look festive in our 1-quart Utensil™ Crock?

CARAMEL BUBBLE BREAD

makes one 8x8-inch square pan

Ingredients:
- Two 1-pound pieces frozen yeast bread or sweet yeast dough, defrosted
- Flour for rolling dough

Glaze Ingredients:
- ¼ cup pure maple syrup
- 1 tablespoon light corn syrup
- ¼ cup light brown sugar
- 1 tablespoon unsalted butter

Pecan Filling Ingredients:
- ½ cup finely chopped pecans
- ¼ cup granulated sugar
- 2 tablespoons all-purpose flour
- 1 teaspoon cinnamon
- 1 large egg
- 3 tablespoons unsalted butter, softened
- ½ cup raisins, plumped in hot water for 5 minutes and drained

Icing Ingredients:
- 2 tablespoons unsalted butter, melted
- 1 cup confectioners' sugar
- Dash of vanilla extract
- Dash of cream or milk

Instructions:
- Preheat oven to 350°F. Lightly butter an 8-inch square baking dish or, if you want to remove the bread from the pan once it is baked, line with buttered parchment paper.
- For the glaze, combine all ingredients in a small heavy-bottomed pan. Over medium heat, stir to dissolve the sugar. Bring to a boil, turn the heat down and simmer 3 minutes. Remove from the heat and cool.
- Press the 2 pieces of defrosted dough together. Lightly dust a work surface with flour and roll the dough into a 12x16-inch rectangle. If the dough does not stretch easily, let it rest for a few minutes before trying again.

- In a mixing bowl, blend together all pecan filling ingredients except for the raisins. Spread the filling evenly over the rolled dough. Sprinkle with raisins. Roll up the dough starting with the 16-inch edge. Seal the dough by pinching the edges together.
- Cut the roll lengthwise into two strips. Cut each half into 2-inch pieces.
- Pour ⅓ of the glaze into the bottom of the prepared pan. Tuck half of the dough pieces into the pan. Pour more glaze over the first layer of dough. Cover with another layer of dough pieces and drizzle with the remaining glaze.
- Cover loosely with aluminum foil and bake 35 minutes. Remove foil and bake another 10 to 15 minutes or until the center of the bread is fully baked. Transfer to a cooling rack.
- For the icing, combine all ingredients in a bowl and mix until smooth.
- Once the bread has completely cooled, drizzle with the icing.

CITRUS SQUARES

makes one 9x13-inch pan

Filling Ingredients:
- 3 large egg yolks
- One 14-ounce can sweetened condensed milk
- Zest of ½ orange and 2 tablespoons juice
- Zest of 1 lemon and 4 tablespoons juice
- Zest of 1 lime and 6 tablespoons juice
- 1 recipe Bar Cookie Crust

Topping Ingredients:
- 1 cup sweetened flaked coconut
- 2 large egg whites
- Pinch of salt
- ⅓ cup plus 1 tablespoon granulated sugar
- 1 teaspoon cornstarch
- 1 teaspoon pure vanilla extract

Instructions:
- Prepare 1 recipe of the Bar Cookie Crust. Preheat oven to 350°F.
- Combine all filling ingredients in a medium mixing bowl and whisk until smooth. Pour the filling over the pre-baked crust and return to the oven for 6 to 7 minutes, or until the filling is just set.
- For the topping, place the coconut on a baking pan and toast it at 350°F for 5 to 8 minutes or until it turns a light golden color. Cool.
- Place the egg whites and salt in the bowl of an electric mixer and beat on medium speed until the whites are frothy, about 2 minutes. Begin to add the sugar, 1 tablespoon at a time, and continue to beat until the whites are thick and hold firm peaks. Beat in the cornstarch and then the vanilla just to incorporate. Fold in the cooled, toasted coconut.
- Gently spread the topping evenly over the lemon filling. Bake at 350°F for 10 to 15 minutes or until the meringue topping sets and turns a light golden color. Once cool, cut into bars. Store any leftovers in the refrigerator.

BAR COOKIE CRUST
makes one 9x13-inch crust

Ingredients:
- 1 cup (2 sticks) unsalted butter, chilled
- ½ cup confectioners' sugar
- 2 cups all-purpose flour

Instructions:
- Preheat oven to 350°F. Mist a 9x13-inch pan with vegetable oil spray.
- Beat the butter and sugar in the bowl of an electric mixer until smooth and creamy. Add the flour and mix until just incorporated; the dough should just begin to form a ball.
- Press the dough in an even layer over the bottom of the prepared pan. Prick the dough all over with a fork. Bake for 20 minutes, or until the surface of the crust is lightly golden brown.

WHOOPIE PIES

makes 3½ dozen pies

Ingredients:
- 1½ cups vegetable shortening
- 3 cups granulated sugar
- 3 large eggs
- 1 tablespoon pure vanilla extract
- 1½ cups cocoa
- 6 cups all-purpose flour
- 1 tablespoon salt
- 1 tablespoon baking soda
- 1½ cups hot water
- ½ cup whole milk
- 1 recipe Cream Filling

Instructions:
- Preheat oven to 400°F. Lightly mist several baking sheets with vegetable oil.
- Cream the shortening in the bowl of an electric mixer for 2 minutes. Add the sugar and beat until creamy, 1 to 2 minutes.
- Add the eggs and vanilla and mix just until incorporated.
- Sift together the cocoa, flour and salt in a large mixing bowl.

- Combine the baking soda and hot water and stir to dissolve.
- On low speed, add the dry ingredients in three additions, alternating with the water/soda mixture. Stop the mixer and scrape the sides and the bottom of the bowl. Add the milk and mix just until incorporated.
- Drop heaping tablespoons of the batter 2 inches apart onto the prepared baking sheets. Place the sheets on the middle rack in the oven and bake 8 to 10 minutes.
- Cool the cookies on racks. Place a generous tablespoon of Cream Filling between 2 cookies.

CREAM FILLING

Ingredients:
- 3 large egg whites
- 6 cups confectioners' sugar
- 5 tablespoons whole milk
- 1 tablespoon vanilla extract
- 1½ cups vegetable shortening

Instructions:
- In the bowl of an electric mixer, whip the egg whites until stiff. Add the sugar, milk and vanilla extract and mix until combined.
- In another bowl, cream the shortening. Add the egg mixture and combine until smooth.

· Whoopie! ·

Whoopie Pies are one of Tami Longaberger's favorites, with a history that goes way back to her childhood. Tami first shared this recipe in *At Home With The Longabergers*, a recipe book written by Rachel Longaberger in 1989. Tami's not the only one who likes Whoopie Pies; they were big sellers at a bake sale held at our home office in Newark, Ohio. The bake sale was sponsored by our "Fun Committee," which makes sure we all receive our daily requirement of 25% fun!

Want to know the names of all the Longaberger originals shown in this book?

BELOW WE'VE IDENTIFIED EVERY LONGABERGER BASKET AND TABLETOP ACCESSORY FEATURED IN THE PRECEDING PAGES, FOLLOWED BY A LIST OF BASKETS WE USED MOST OFTEN THROUGHOUT THIS BOOK. THESE ARE THE BASKETS WE COULDN'T LIVE WITHOUT, AND WE KNOW YOU CAN'T EITHER!

PARTY PLANNING

BASKETS

- Address™ Basket – rolodex cards
- Small Boardwalk™ Basket – handbag
- Small Corner Basket – desk top accessories
- Large Desktop™ Basket – invitation supplies
- Ice Bucket Basket (August 2003 feature) – cleaning supplies
- Note Pal™ Basket – note paper
- Kiddie Purse - coupons

WINTER

A Warm Holiday Welcome

BASKETS

- Small Berry Basket – cocktail napkins
- 9" Bowl Basket – White Cheddar Pepper Scones
- 13" Bowl Basket (with protector, pottery Large Pasta Bowl and 1-pint Salt™ Crock) – Shrimp and cocktail sauce (ice in the protector keeps the pasta bowl chilled)
- Bread Basket – Cranberry Orange Nut Bread
- Business Card Basket – sugar packets
- Cracker Basket – assorted crackers
- Small Gatehouse® Basket – in center of wreath with a poinsettia
- Small Gathering Basket – Rectangular Tray filled with White Chocolate Pecan Fudge (fudge refills are inside the basket)
- Pen Pal™ Basket – flatware
- Salt & Pepper™ Basket
- Small Serving Tray Basket – Smoked Salmon Spirals

WOVEN TRADITIONS® POTTERY

- Small Dessert Bowls – Longaberger Homestead® Bread Pudding
- Cake Plates – sliced turkey, Crabmeat Remoulade
- Small Covered Dish – (on a cake plate) – Crabmeat Remoulade
- 1-pint Salt™ Crocks – sauces, flatware
- Divided Dish – nuts and olives
- Large Pasta Bowl – shrimp
- Dinner Plates
- Rectangular Tray – Fruit and Cheese
- Salt & Pepper Shakers
- Sugar Bowl & Creamer Set
- Votive Cups – votive candles

TABLETOP

- American Holly™ Mugs
- American Holly™ Vases
- Woven Traditions™ Flatware Serving pieces

FABRIC

- American Holly™
- Solids: Paprika and Ivy

METALWORKS

- Small Baker's Rack™ - coffee bar
- Divided Dish Pedestal and WoodCrafts Shelf – Divided Dish
- Mixing Bowl Stand with WoodCrafts Shelves – Buffet Serving Station
- Rectangular Pedestal Stand – Rectangular Tray

FEATURE

- Glass Cake Stand (Sept – Dec 2003) – Brie

A Good Morning

BASKETS

- 9" Bowl Basket – Banana Crumb Muffins and Citrus Bowl with Vanilla Yogurt Sauce
- Small Serving Tray Basket – holds Mugs, Tarragon™ Booking Basket with Crock Coasters
- Tall Tissue™ Basket – 4-inch pots of poinsettias
- Tarragon™ Booking Basket - coasters

WOVEN TRADITIONS® POTTERY

- 8X8 Baking Dish – Baked Apple French Toast
- Small Dessert Bowls
- 2-Quart Covered Casserole – Savory Breakfast Casserole
- Creamer
- 1-pint Salt™ Crock – 8-ounce tub of margarine
- Single Crock Lid/Coaster – coasters
- Mugs
- Luncheon Plates
- Votive Cups – candles

TABLETOP

- American Holly™ Vase
- Woven Traditions™ 12-Ounce Tumblers
- Woven Traditions™ Flatware

FABRIC

- American Holly™
- Solids: Paprika and Ivy

Brrr! Hooray! Snow Day!

BASKETS

- 7" Bowl Basket – oyster crackers, eggs, butter
- 9" Bowl Basket – Crystal Snowball Cookies
- 11" Bowl Baskets – pretzels and chips
- Button Basket – 16-ounce container of whipped cream

- Cilantro™ Booking Basket - Snow Friend
- Cracker Baskets – flatware, Oatmeal Apple Toffee Drops
- Darning Basket – Marshmallow Snowmen
- Extra Small Gatehouse® Basket – tissues, lip balm
- Medium Market – on the sled
- Paper Tray Basket with 6-Way Divided Protector – napkins, teaspoons, hot chocolate toppings
- Small Serving Tray – cornbread in 9X13 Baking Dish
- Work-A-Round™ Basket – snow covered clothes

WOVEN TRADITIONS® POTTERY
- 9X13 Baking Dish – Cozy Cornbread
- Cereal Bowls
- Small Dessert Bowl – Chili for little ones
- 1-pint Salt™ Crocks – Chili condiments
- Mugs – Old-Fashioned Hot Cocoa
- Dinner Plates
- Soup Tureen – Chili

TABLETOP
- Woven Traditions™ Flatware

FABRIC
- Solid Indigo

METALWORKS
- Small Baker's Rack™ - Buffet Serving Station
- Paper Tray Stand with WoodCrafts Shelves – Hot Chocolate Station

FEATURE
- Blue Ribbon™ One Quart Canning Jars (May 2003 Feature)– cornbread dry ingredients

SPRING

Easter Joy

BASKETS
- American Craft Originals™ Casserole Basket – Easter eggs
- 9" Bowl Basket – Easter eggs
- Cake Basket with Wood Riser – mugs
- Medium Gathering Basket – Almond Cream Cake in 9X13 Baking Dish
- Salt & Pepper™ Basket
- Spring™ Basket – Easter Basket

WOVEN TRADITIONS® POTTERY
- 9X13 Baking Dish – Almond Cream Cake
- Creamer – Mustard Sauce
- 1-pint Salt™ Crocks – tub of margarine, Fresh Pineapple Sauce, daffodils
- 1-quart Utensil™ Crock – 4-inch pots of daffodils
- Mugs – Little Chickie Pudding Cups
- Grandma Bonnie's™ Pie Plate – Au Gratin Potatoes
- Bread Plates
- Dinner Plates
- Luncheon Plates – Spring Salad with Sherry Vinaigrette

- Rectangular Tray – Glazed Ham with Mustard Sauce
- Salt & Pepper Shakers
- Votive Cups – Votive Cup Place Cards

AMERICAN CRAFT ORIGINALS® POTTERY
- 11" Bowl – decorative grass
- Covered Casserole – Carrots and Sugar Snap Peas in Chive Butter

TABLETOP
- Woven Traditions™ 17-ounce Tumblers
- Woven Traditions™ Flatware

FABRIC
- Cornflower Plaid™

METALWORKS
- Rectangular Pedestal Stand – Rectangular Tray

Mom's Big Day

BASKETS
- American Craft Originals™ Coaster Basket – Pitcher
- 9" Bowl Basket – oranges
- Cracker Basket – three Votive Cups filled with toppings
- Small Serving Tray Basket – tray with coffee, berries and cream for Mom
- Sewing Notions™ Basket – filled with pansies

WOVEN TRADITIONS® POTTERY
- Small Dessert Bowls – brown sugar, syrup, coffee beans, berries
- Butter Dish
- Creamers – syrup and cream
- Mugs
- Bread Plates – Sweet Heart Toast
- Dinner Plates – Simple Surprise Pancakes
- Votive Cups – toppings and flowers

AMERICAN CRAFT ORIGINALS® POTTERY
- Pitcher

TABLETOP
- Woven Traditions™ 12-ounce Tumblers
- Woven Traditions™ Flatware

FABRIC
- Botanical Fields™

Spring Showers

BASKETS
- Small Berry Basket – cocktail napkins
- Business Card Basket – mints
- Corner Basket – rolled napkins
- Medium Gathering Basket – party favors
- Pen Pal™ Basket – Woven Traditions™ Flatware
- Serve It Up!™ Basket – Woven Traditions™ 17-ounce Tumblers
- Tiny Tote™ Basket – lilacs
- Small Oval Waste Basket – lilacs
- Work-A-Round™ Basket – gifts

WOVEN TRADITIONS® POTTERY
- Small Dessert Bowls – nuts
- Cake Plates – Mini Fresh Fruit Tarts and Garden Party Hat Cake
- Large Milk Pitcher – beverage refills
- Bread Plates
- Dinner Plates – on Wrought Iron Stand with Tea Sandwiches
- Luncheon Plates
- Sugar Bowl

AMERICAN CRAFT ORIGINALS® POTTERY
- 11" Bowl – ice
- 10" Bowl– Asparagus Salad with Champagne Dressing

TABLETOP
- Woven Traditions™ 17-ounce Tumblers
- Woven Traditions™ Flatware

FABRIC
- Spring Floral™

METALWORKS
- Two-Pie Server

SUMMER

Friends and Food Alfresco

BASKETS
- Medium Boardwalk™ Basket – Flowers
- 7" Bowl Basket – Summer Potpourri
- 9" Bowl Basket – tomatoes
- 11" Bowl Basket – zucchini
- 13" Bowl Basket – peppers
- Bread Basket – Grilled Garlic Toasts
- Salt & Pepper™ Basket
- Tiny Tote™ Basket – flowers
- Umbrella Basket – croquet mallets

WOVEN TRADITIONS® POTTERY
- Butter Dish
- Cereal Bowls – Roasted Red Pepper Gazpacho
- Small Dessert Bowls – party favors, candles and Toasted Croutons
- Cake Plate – Grilled Vegetables with Crumbled Feta
- 1-pint Salt™ Crocks
- Single Crock Lid/Coasters - candles
- Divided Dish – Petals and Pottery Centerpiece
- Dinner Plates
- Rectangular Tray – Grilled Halibut with Chopped Olive Tapenade
- Salt & Pepper Shakers
- Votive Cups

TABLETOP
- Woven Traditions™ 12-ounce Tumblers – votive candles, Fresh Berry Parfaits
- Woven Traditions™ 17-ounce Tumblers – beverages
- Pint Size Pillar Scented Candles – Vanilla
- Woven Traditions™ Flatware

FABRIC
- Fruit Medley™
- Solid Paprika

METALWORKS
- Bowl Stand – Bowl Baskets
- Dessert Bowl Caddy – Small Dessert Bowls with votive candles
- Divided Dish Pedestal – Divided Dish
- Rectangular Pedestal Stand – Rectangular Tray
- Round Pedestal Stand with WoodCrafts Shelf – Cake Plate
- Umbrella Stand – Umbrella Basket with crouquet mallets

What a Blast!

BASKETS
- Proudly American™ Button Baskets – 6-inch round paper dessert plates, sidewalk chalk
- Proudly American™ Cracker Basket – crackers
- Proudly American™ Darning Basket – 9-inch round paper plates
- Proudly American™ Medium Gathering Basket – project supplies
- Proudly American™ Salt and Pepper™ Basket – (Collectors Club April 2003 Feature)
- Proudly American™ Small Picnic Basket – Polaroid cameras
- Proudly American™ Small Picnic Basket with wood riser - pies
- Proudly American™ Spring™ Basket – napkins, plastic utensils, corn on the cob
- Proudly American™ Small Wash Day™ Basket – water balloons
- Bagel Basket – Golden Pound Cakes, onions, tomatoes and lettuce
- 11" Bowl Basket – Overnight Vegetable Salad
- 13" Bowl Basket – Dilly Garden Salad
- Cake Basket with wood riser – 1-Pint Salt™ Crocks filled with fruit and whipped cream
- Medium Market Basket – chips
- Serve It Up!™ Basket – vegetables and dip
- Small Serving Tray Basket – Whoopie Pies
- Work-A-Round™ Basket – ice and bottled water

WOVEN TRADITIONS® POTTERY
- 9X13 Baking Dish – Fiesta Taco Dip
- Small Dessert Bowls – dip in vegetable tray, hamburger toppings
- Cake Plate – hamburgers
- 2-Quart Covered Casserole – Orzo Salad
- 1-pint Salt™ Crocks – fruit and whipped cream
- Large 10" Mixing Bowl – Potato Salad
- Grandma Bonnie's™ Pie Plate – Peach Cobbler
- Salt & Pepper Shakers

PROUDLY AMERICAN® POTTERY
- Platter – hot dogs
- Casserole – Amish Baked Beans

TABLETOP
- Woven Traditions™ Flatware

FABRIC
• Old Glory™
• Solids: Paprika and Indigo

METALWORKS
• Dessert Bowl Caddy – Small Dessert Bowls filled with hamburger toppings

FALL

Halloween Fun

BASKETS
• Corner Basket – Crunchy Munchies and Ghost Toasties
• Cracker Baskets – cookies, paints
• Darning Basket – 9-inch round paper plates
• Large Fruit Basket – yarn
• Medium Market Basket – Slugs & Bugs Goody Bags
• Paper Tray Basket – construction paper
• Serve It Up!™ Basket – Nutty Caramel Apples, Pumpkin Face Cupcakes
• Work-A-Round™ Basket – pumpkins
• Large Work Load™ Basket – juice boxes

WOVEN TRADITIONS® POTTERY
• Small Dessert Bowls – Pumpkin Face Cupcakes
• 1-quart Utensil™ Crock – scissors
• Small 6" Mixing Bowls – icing
• Large Milk Pitchers – juice
• Dinner Plates – Make-A-Face Pizzas
• Luncheon Plates
• Votive Cups – crayons

TABLETOP
• Woven Traditions™ 12-ounce Tumblers
• Woven Traditions™ Flatware

FABRIC
• Pumpkin Patch™
• Solids: Sage, Ivy and Butternut

METALWORKS
• Two-Pie Server – Dinner Plates filled with Make-A-Face Pizzas

Always Good to Go

BASKETS
• Bagel Basket – peanuts
• Large Boardwalk™ Basket – Stadium Blankets
• 9" Bowl Basket – Pretzel Mix
• 11" Bowl Basket – Chilled Penne Salad
• Bread Basket – Garden Crunch Sandwiches
• Cake Basket – paper plates, cups and napkins
• Medium Gathering Basket – Alsatian Chicken Sandwiches with Caramelized Onion-Apple Mayonnaise
• Medium Market Baskets – chips, flowers
• Large Picnic Basket – ice and drinks
• Serve It Up!™ Basket – Vegetable Trays with Caesar Dip

• Small Serving Tray Basket – Fresh Fruit Skewers, Chocolate Pecan Bars

WOVEN TRADITIONS® POTTERY
• 9X13 Baking Dish – Chocolate Pecan Bars
• Large Milk Pitcher – flowers

FABRIC
• Solids: Paprika and Sage
• Orchard Park Plaid™

A Traditional Feast

BASKETS
• 13" Bowl Basket – bread
• Small Gatehouse® Basket – Bountiful Chair Baskets
• Medium Market Basket
• Salt & Pepper™ Basket

WOVEN TRADITIONS® POTTERY
• Butter Dish
• Small Dessert Bowls – Zesty Orange Cranberry Sauce
• 2-Quart Covered Casserole – Chestnut Dressing, Baked Maple Sweet Potatoes
• Small Covered Dish – Gravy
• Mugs – Dessert Buffet
• Grandma Bonnie's™ Pie Plate – Apple Blackberry Crumble Pie, Rachel's Favorite Pumpkin Pie
• Bread Plates – Dessert Buffet
• Dinner Plates
• Rectangular Tray – Green Beans with Shitake Mushrooms
• Salt & Pepper Shakers
• Turkey Platter – Roasted Turkey

TABLETOP
• Woven Traditions™ 12-ounce Tumblers
• Woven Traditions™ Flatware

FABRIC
• Falling Leaves™
• Solids: Sage and Oatmeal

METALWORKS
• Rectangular Pedestal Stand – Rectangular Tray
• Two-Pie Server – pies on Dessert Buffet

WOODCRAFTS
• Butcher Block Stand

ANYTIME AT ALL

It's A Zoo Birthday Party

BASKETS
• Bagel Basket – Ants On A Log
• Bread Basket – Crispy Critter Drumsticks
• Medium Market Basket – party favors
• Row Your Boat™ Basket – bananas
• Saffron™ Booking Basket – Nuts and Berries Trail Mix
• Medium Storage Solutions Basket – party gear

WOVEN TRADITIONS® POTTERY
- Small Dessert Bowls – dipping sauces
- Mugs – Cupcakes with Shortbread Cookie Toppers
- Large Pasta Bowl – Speared Ham and Cheese Chunks
- Dinner Plates
- Luncheon Plates

TABLETOP
- Woven Traditions™ Flatware

FABRIC
- Paprika Plaid™
- Solids: Paprika and Sage

METALWORKS
- Round Pedestal Stand – Large Pasta Bowl

Red Hot Birthday Fiesta!

BASKETS
- Bagel Basket – Divided Dish with salsa
- 9" Bowl Basket with protector – 1-Quart Casserole with chicken filling and beef filling for tacos
- 11" Bowl Basket – chips
- Bread Basket – taco shells
- Darning Basket – flour tortillas
- Medium Fruit Basket – Santa Fe Salad
- Large Fruit Basket – ice
- Small Gatehouse® Basket – can of whipped cream
- Tiny Tote™ Basket – gerbera daisies

WOVEN TRADITIONS® POTTERY
- Small Dessert Bowls – taco toppings
- 1-Quart Casserole – chicken filling, beef filling
- 2-Quart Casserole Lid – fits on the Darning Basket
- Creamer – salad dressing
- Cresent Dishes – sundae toppings
- 1-pint Salt™ Crocks – teaspoons, ice cream toppings
- 2-quart Pickling™ Crock – tub of ice cream
- Divided Dish – salsas
- Small 6" Mixing Bowl – diced tomatoes
- Large Pasta Bowl – pepper/candle centerpiece
- Dinner Plates

TABLETOP
- Woven Traditions™ Flatware

FABRIC
- Solids: Paprika, Cornflower, Ivy and Butternut

METALWORKS
- Dessert Bowl Caddy –Small Dessert Bowls filled with taco toppings
- Round Pedestal Stand with WoodCrafts shelf – centerpiece, Devil's Food Cake

WOODCRAFTS
- Not-So-Lazy Susan™ - Sundae Station

Goodies For A Good Cause

BASKETS
- Bread Basket (on Small Bakers Rack™) – Chocolate Pecan Bars
- Cake Basket – Caramel Bubble Bread, Devil's Food Cake, and placed on the shelves of the Butcher Block Stand
- Cilantro™ Basket – entry forms
- Corner Baskets – Whoopie Pies, Apples
- Small Corner Baskets – Ohio Buckeyes
- Darning Basket – Shortbread Cookies
- Small Gathering Basket (on Small Bakers Rack™) – Chocolate Pecan Bars
- Medium Gathering Basket – Citrus Squares
- Paper Tray Basket – Iced Sugar Cookies
- Tapered Paper Tray Basket – Iced Sugar Cookies
- Serve It Up!™ Basket – Banana Crumb Muffins, Oatmeal Apple Toffee Drops
- Small Serving Tray Baskets – Nutty Caramel Apples, Cranberry Orange Nut Bread
- Spring™ Basket – paper napkins
- Tall Tissue™ Basket with Lid – drawing box
- Work-A-Round™ Basket – bottled water

WOVEN TRADITIONS® POTTERY
- Single Crock Lid/Coaster –on the Dessert Bowl Caddy with stacked doughnuts
- 1-quart Utensil™ Crock – Dipped Pretzels, Lollipop Trees
- Large 10" Mixing Bowls – Nuts and Berries Trail Mix

FABRIC
- Solid Paprika

METALWORKS
- Small Bakers Rack™ with WoodCrafts Shelves – Chocolate Pecan Bars
- Corner Stands with WoodCraft Shelves – Apples, Crystal Snowball Cookies, Whoopie Pies, Banana Crumb Muffins
- Small Corner Stand – Ohio Buckeyes
- Dessert Bowl Caddy – stacked doughnuts resting on 1-Pint Lid
- Divided Dish Pedestal with WoodCrafts Shelf – Small Serving Tray with Nutty Caramel Apples
- Mixing Bowl Stands with WoodCrafts Shelves – Ohio Buckeyes, White Chocolate Pecan Fudge, Nuts and Berries Trail Mix
- Paper Tray Stands with WoodCrafts Shelves – Iced Sugar Cookies

WOODCRAFTS
- Butcher Block Stand

MOST OFTEN USED BASKETS IN ENTERTAINING WITH LONGABERGER

9" Bowl Basket	Medium Gathering Basket
11" Bowl Basket	Medium Market Basket
Bread Basket	Salt & Pepper™ Basket
Cracker Basket	Serve It Up!™
Darning Basket	Small Serving Tray

Recipe Index

P
Pantry Chili, 53
Pastry Cream, 91
Peach Cobbler, 116
Pesto Butter, 89
Pie Dough, 150
Potato Salad Dressing, 114
Pumpkin Face Cupcakes, 128

R
Rachel's Favorite Pumpkin Pie, 151
Roasted Red Pepper Gazpacho with Toasted Croutons, 100
Roasted Turkey with Gravy, 145
Royal Icing, 50

S
Santa Fe Salad, 172
Sautéed Apples, 42
Savory Breakfast Casserole, 41
Sherry Vinaigrette, 69
Shortbread Cookies, 182
Simple Surprise Pancakes, 78
Smoked Salmon Spirals, 32
Smoked Turkey Breast Sandwiches, 28
Sparkling Raspberry Lemonade, 86
Speared Ham and Cheese Chunks, 162
Spicy Chicken Tacos, 173
Spicy Plum Sauce, 28
Spring Salad with Sherry Vinaigrette, 69
Streusel Topping, 150
Sweet Heart Toast, 79

T
Toasted Croutons, 100
Tomato-Basil Tea Sandwiches, 89
Turkey Gravy, 146

V
Vanilla Yogurt Sauce, 44
Vegetable Trays with Caesar Dip, 136
Vegetarian Chili, 54

W
White Cheddar Pepper Scones, 29
White Chocolate Macadamia Nut Fudge, 33
White Chocolate Pecan Fudge, 33
White Chocolate Peppermint Fudge, 33
Whoopie Pies, 185

Z
Zesty Orange Cranberry Sauce, 149

Project Index

A
Autumn Branch Place Cards, 143

B
Block Party Memory Book, 109
Bountiful Chair Baskets, 144

C
Cherry Tomato Place Favors, 97
Chili Pepper Invitations, 169
Christmas Candy Cones, 26

D
Decoupage Frame, 75

E
Easy Bake Sale Banner, 179

F
Feathered Friend Feeder, 40
Fiesta Place Cards, 170
Fun Napkin Folds, 65

G
Garden Party Hat Cake, 85

H
Handcrafted Piñatas, 171

J
Jungle Leaf Invitations, 157
Jungle Table, 159

L
Little Chickie Place Cards, 64
Little House Invitations, 107

M
Magnetic Photo Collage, 133
Marshmallow Snowmen, 50

O
Open House Invitations, 25

P
Paper Rose Shower Invitations, 83
Party Animal Bags, 158
Patriotic T-shirt Decorating, 108
Petals and Pottery Centerpiece, 98
Presentable Price Signs, 179
Prize Winning Lollipops, 179
Promise Boxes, 76

S
Slithering Snake Party Favors, 160
Slugs & Bugs Goody Bags, 125
Snow Day Invitations, 49
Socked-In Snow Friends, 52
Spooky Spider Invitations, 123
Spooky Spider Place Cards, 124
Summer Potpourri, 99

T
Terribly Crafty Pumpkin Heads, 126
Tissue Paper Decorations, 84
Treat-Wrapping Techniques, 180

V
Votive Cup Place Cards, 63

To learn more about our company and to get in touch with an Independent Longaberger® Sales Consultant, call our Customer Referral Department at 1-800-966-0374, or visit us at www.longaberger.com.